DOWN

the

GINNEL

More
Shoddy Town Tales

by
Fred Butler

illustrated by Graham Kaye

FAB Publications

First published in 2002
by
FAB Publications
Eastfield House
Flash Lane
Mirfield
West Yorkshire
WF14 0PU
Tel/Fax 01924 492249

ISBN 0-9540683-1-9

Illustrations by Graham Kaye
Brighouse West Yorkshire 01484 712752

Printed in Great Britain by
Central Publishing Services
www.centralpublishing.co.uk

Dedicated

to

all Shoddy Town folk

throughout the world,

wherever they may be

CONTENTS

Introduction

****

TO BEGIN WITH ...

By the time I was eleven years old, I'd begun to think that I was a bit of a nomad. I was born in Beeston, Notts, shortly after the Normandy Landings of the Second World War and my early life was a trek the length and breadth of the country. Whilst my father gradually improved his foundryman's skills and, at the same time, our family's welfare, so we had to trail after him. I'd settle down nicely, thank you very much, at the local nursery or junior school, make friends, play in the sand-pit and enjoy the afternoon naps they made us take at infant school in those days.

Then suddenly, it would all go haywire.

Every two or three years, my dad would come home from work and announce that we were moving - lock stock and barrel - to some place I'd never heard of, where he'd secured a better-paid job. By the time the winter snows of 1956 had settled on the landscape of England, I'd lived [and attended schools] in Wolverhampton [Staffs.], Peterborough [Northants] and Stroud [Glos.]. Finally, in the glorious summer sunshine of 1957, we came to rest in Liversedge [West Yorkshire.] So the Heavy Woollen District became my home, and my roots became firmly implanted in the rich, brass-ridden muck of the Shoddy Towns.

Labouring under the severe handicap of not being born a Yorkshireman, I did my adolescent best to convince anyone whom I might meet that I was, in fact, a native of "God's Own County". And, dare I say it, I met with some measure of success. I joined the team and rapidly learned to talk the talk and to walk the walk of a dyed-in-the-blood Shoddy Town lad. Nowadays, I am readily taken for a native of Batley, Dewsbury, Heckmondwike or even Cleckheaton!

A plod through the very traditional Batley Grammar School of the 50's and 60's provided me with six GCE O Levels, three A levels, and a fertile stock of legendary tales. More importantly, however, I received some life-influencing careers advice.

My Sixth Form form-master revealed to me [and one or two others in my form] that we were not bright enough to attend university. "So you'd better go to college and become teachers," he pontificated from his lofty academic perch with a dainty white handkerchief tucked up his worldly-wise sleeve.

Accepting unquestioningly such learned Oxford University advice, that's exactly what we did.

At the country's expense, I attended Goldsmiths' College, London, for three years' worth of college life. I met a lot of new people, drank a lot of flat beer, played a great deal of football and came out into the big wide world as a qualified teacher.

Of course, there was only one place in which I wanted to work. At a time when teaching jobs grew on trees, I returned to the Shoddy Towns, where I had the choice of several posts. My first was at Batley Boys' High School in 1966; my second was at Earlsheaton School, Dewsbury, where I remained for 28 years.

And what a wise move *that* turned out to be!

Before I knew it, I was playing football for Wheelwright

Old Boys, acting daft at the Dewsbury Arts Group, taking Shoddy Town kids on camping trips and meeting local folk about their daily business. Amongst all this, I'm supposed to be educating the children in my charge. Looking back through my life-telescope of time, it was the other way about - *they* were educating *me*, so I'm pleased to offer this second collection of tales for their enjoyment.

Perhaps some of those former pupils might recognise themselves. Most of them have heard the tales before, in different guise, for they all featured in my morning assemblies.

In its original form, each of my stories contained a moral which I attempted to use as a very righteous teaching point. But the tides of time have long-since washed all that away. Nowadays, I prefer to recall those events as part of the weekly ego-trip in which I selfishly indulged and which masqueraded under the title of "assembly".

But please forget the moralising and enjoy the humour of those instructive life-moments. They've all figured large in my journey Down the Ginnel of Very Happy Memories. As a result, they are all vital ingredients in this second set of Shoddy Town Tales.

***

Fred Butler
February 2002

FAILURE

From an early age, it was suggested to me very subtly by various members of the family that I had to be a winner. Not in a selfish, win-at-all-costs, I-am-the-centre-of-the Universe kind of winner. No, but they always dropped lead-weight hints that I was expected to do well in order to uphold the family honour. And nowhere was this more evident than in the field of education.

Just as with most kids of my generation, passing the 11+ exam and gaining a place at the Grammar School was seen as a feather in our parents' caps, and not necessarily any indication of how brainy *we* happened to be. All sorts of inducements were dangled temptingly in our final junior school year to "pass the exam". Success for *us* meant that our mums and dads could walk proudly down the street, puffing out their chests and crowing to everybody: "Hey, dusta know, my lad's offter t'grammar schooil..."

In my case, I was promised a *brand new* Triumph Palm Beach bicycle with straight handle-bars and dyno-hub lighting. In the days of mucking about on a second-hand, sit-up-and-beg Elswick Shopper, this was like the rubbing of Alladin's Lamp, so there was every incentive to study my socks off and pass that pesky exam.

At Uplands County Primary school in Stroud, my Gloucestershire spring and summer of 1955 was dominated by practice test upon practice test. We were being prepared for the big day of The Exam which came and went like any other in the long, blissful days of an idyllic childhood. Many weeks after all the tests had faded from our memories, there followed hours of earnest playground discussion about the future. None of us, it appeared, wanted to be a "grammar bug" and I vividly remember swearing on my honour to Micky Morgan, Donald Beard and Mervyn Scrivens that I would *definitely* go to the "Tech" with all my mates.

The day of judgement finally arrives and tall, balding Mr Skinner, headmaster at our rural junior school, looms at the front of our class and announces the names of the kids who would be going to the grammar school. Sure enough, mine is on the list and my reward was duly delivered - a beautiful, gleaming blue and yellow Palm Beach velocipede...

So September sees me dressed in a smart black blazer and a pair of long-short grey trousers with a razor-sharp crease as I make my lonesome way down Farmhill, through Paganhill and on to the Marling Grammar School. I desperately wanted to be with my mates at the Technical School across the other side of town, so for a month or two, I am less than happy. Still, at least I had a new bike upon which to while away the long summer evenings...

And then my world is shattered even further when my Dad announces that he has got a new job in Yorkshire and we are to move post-haste "up North". I shed many tears as the removal van pulls up outside our new home in Liversedge and I begin life anew in the Heavy Woollen District.

After what seemed an age and a not-too-unpleasant enforced holiday from any educational establishment of any kind, my mother informs me that she has arrived at a decision. I will be attending Batley Grammar School for *Boys*, even though there are two perfectly good mixed grammar schools virtually on our doorstep. However, not being of a questioning nature, I accept my fate and present myself at those hallowed portals half way up Carlinghow Hill, ready to join the educational rat-race...

I am ushered into the hallway of a temporary classroom where I am interviewed by a be-gowned Mr Marsden. He takes my eleven-year old breath away by conducting our entire consultation in French which comes as something of a shock. I answer all his questions with stammering ineptness. Previous learning deserts me, I become a foolish stuttering wreck, and my academic ability is assessed as "M" [for mediocre]. I am thus allocated a place in the Alpha-form.

So now, the starting stalls are raised and the rat-race begins. And what a race it turned out to be!

Like most grammar schools of the 50's, Batley thrived on the first past the post, competitive process. At the start of their "race" through the grammar school, all boys went into the educational starting stalls as indicated by their 11+ results. These stalls were called forms and there were three distinct levels - A, Alpha and B. As the race panned out, those who fell by the wayside were left way behind and this meant relegation to a lower class of race next time out.

If you consistently came bottom of the monthly mark lists, and if you didn't do well enough in the end-of-term exams, it meant demotion to a lower form for the coming academic year.

So you left behind all your bosom pals as you sank down the educational ladder and you hit rock-bottom - unless you were in the B-form. There being nowhere to go from there, you were asked politely if you would like to try Healey Boys' School or anywhere else they might take you on.

Now that kind of system is fine if you're a bright, clever A-form swot who wouldn't recognise Failure if it jumped up your trouser leg and bit you in the bum.

But if you're a steady, middle of the road Alpha-form boy who grunts and groans his way through homework, and struggles nightly with the complexities of Pythagoras Theorem, the prospect of failure and demotion was awesomely terrifying. And if there was one thing that we Alpha-form lads were *all* certain about, it was that we could *not* face the prospect of going home to Mummy and Daddy and telling them that we were going down to the B-form.

Fear of failure was also reinforced by the fact that, in the eyes of the BGS establishment, failing any kind of test was a carnal sin, deserving of Very Severe Punishment. No doubt the Rack, perhaps a couple of Thumb-screws or even Death by Hanging appealed to our masters' sense of justice, but since such measures were denied to them by a fairly humane, post-war educational regime, they had to settle for the Saturday Morning Detention. Failure to achieve $^7/_{10}$ for any test meant the automatic award of a "Sat'day", and was to be avoided at all costs.

So this is where the fun starts...

Rather than devoting all our waking hours and adolescent energies towards *learning* our work in order to pass all those lousy tests and thus stay out of detention, we devised an admirable array of tactics for beating the system. Such ploys went under the collective name of "cribbing", but they involved much more than merely copying from your mate's open, unguarded exercise book.

The unstated reward was avoiding the "drop" to the B-form, and this awesome spectre of failure tested our Grammar school artfulness to its maximum. Often wantonly neglecting our homework, we spent hour upon hour devising devious ploys to gain the required $^7/_{10}$. This meant having to hastily copy missed homework from Form Swot's book in the cloakroom before the 9am bell.

Our school day would then unfold its store of educational treasures for our delight, each lesson ending with the dreaded announcement of homework learning for a test the next day. So what did those masters expect of us? Did they really think that we would spend a long summer evening committing material for half-a-dozen tests to adolescent memory? Arriving home, we were all completely devastated by the prospect of learning page after dreary page of factual information for several tests the next day. So we took out insurance to preserve our Alpha-form status...

A very small piece of paper can be folded three or four times and inserted under your wrist-watch. If you write in sufficiently miniscule letters, and if you're prepared to spend an hour or two the night before squinting at the end of your pencil, you can create several such sheets. Throughout the following day, these will be your very own Information Retrieval System.

As each test dawns, you're brimming with confidence, but

you don't show it to your mates. Maintaining a dour, poker-face, you go into the starting blocks for the first test of the day and the master prepares to baffle you with his academic set of questions. It is a fairly simple job to slyly lift your watch away from your wrist and slide the miniscule scrap of paper under your exercise book.

So, in matters about which you don't know a thing - which is most of the test - you have a tiny consultation document which will see you through. For the first lesson's History test, there is a successful outcome as you cunningly access a list of facts and dates about the 1832 Reform Act and the Corn Laws.

Next up is Maths. Pythagoras Theorem, Cosine Rules, Calculation of areas of a right angled triangle - it's all there, under the watch strap on a freshly inserted "crib-sheet". French is a piece of cake - all those verbs and vocabulary lists readily to hand whenever the question is put; and remembering Chemistry formulae presents no problem at all.

You attain the magic 70% pass mark across the board, guffaw at the chumps who have ended up with a BGS-committed Saturday morning, and heave a sigh of relief at the preservation of your status when the end-of-term mark lists are posted on the green-backed form notice-board.

Desperate to maintain our position in the middle-educational order of the Alpha-form, we used several other successful methods of "cribbing". I can unequivocally vouch for the positive outcomes derived from several *modi operandi*, having had personal experience in the employment thereof...

Properly regarded, limbs can provide a very useful tool

for cribbing. An arm or a leg, bright pink in its first flush of adolescent development, furnishes an effective background for tiny biro-written characters - the insurance information against failure. Indeed, an entire syllabus can be written up just above the knee and even leaves some room for good luck messages!

The end-of-term examinations arrive, the results of which will be absolutely vital in determining your form group for the next academic year. Our parents scratch their heads in wonder as we *insist* on a nightly bath. Well, you had to wash off today's information and prepare the limb for tomorrow's Physics exam, so there was no time to lose. These were desperate measures to cater for a desperate situation, and succes was vital.

Look across the silent summer examination classroom of 1959. See the afternoon sun beating down on the earnestly bent backs of 4 Alpha as they sweat their way through Boyle's Law and the principle of Fulcrum and Load. Notice several secretively rolled-up trouser-legs and observe many sneakily-surreptitious glances below the desk. Yes, we were all at it, each boy cunningly trawling the surface of his pink thigh for the required morsel of vital educational information.

Another vital pre-requisite for an effective crib-sheet is a stylish shirt. Double cuffs, fastened with links swiped from your Dad's drawer, can be opened out and completed in detail on the reverse side the night before. During the test/exam, under the cover of the desk-top, it was easy to undo the cuff-link and unfold the cuff to reveal all. The masters must have wondered - as did our parents - why it was that during examination time, our dress standards improved dramatically. To us lads, it was obvious, wasn't it? All those boys in the form who were dressed smartly were up to no good with their crib-sheets ready-prepared.

So we merrily trundled our way through our educational careers, never coming "top of the class" [that would give the game away, wouldn't it?] and never coming bottom. As long as we didn't *fail*, that was all that mattered. We wouldn't have to face our parents or our peers with the fact that we'd "gone darn inter t'B-form..."

Needless to say, all educational study involving the liberal use of the crib-sheet method required the expenditure of an enormous amount of time in thought, design and preparation. Rather than waste hours swotting up for exams and tests with the risky spectre of failure at the end if your memory failed you, time was much better spent writing up information in a handy, cribbable form. The ratio of proper swotting as against crib-sheet creation was probably about 2-1, but at the end of it all, *you didn't fail.*

The BGS establishment of the 50's and 60's wielded examinations with all the threat of a Samurai sword to ensure their pupils' success. Keeping ahead of the game with a ready supply of carefully prepared crib-sheets became part of an annual academic battle and it soaked up all our educational energies at exam time.

Our ingenuity was tested to the full as we devised many and varied ways of secreting tiny, folded-up bits of paper about our adolescent bodies. Personal success was determined by the number of ways we "got away with it." It all got very exhausting, especially as you had to plan most of it weeks in advance.

But the finest bit of academic gameship it was my privilege to witness didn't involve the use of any crib-sheets at all. It was spur of the moment stuff and it was perpetrated by Our Hero, Haydn Mitchell one winter's morning in 1958...

Nowadays, anyone who travels around the Shoddy Towns on anything like a regular basis cannot fail to notice that H. Mitchell Car Sales is one of our best known Heavy Woollen District success stories. Its lofty position at the top of Staincliffe reflects the hard graft and business acumen of its owner. In his day, H.Mitchell was a successful sportsman having played Rugby League for Bramley, and such success no doubt spurred on his business career.

However, Haydn is also a life-long friend whose Shoddy Town reputation for fair trade and trustworthiness is second to none. So, looking back over forty-five years of acquaintance, Yours Truly can't help thinking that Haydn's overall fame as a businessman had its roots in the BGS ethos of "Thou must not fail..."

Like the rest of us, Haydn is adept in the use of the crib-sheet. In fact, in his official capacity of Form Bully, he is able to commandeer extra copies of other lads' material for his own personal use. But on this particular occasion, on a dismal, cold February morning, he is absolutely up Batley Beck without a paddle.

A Maths test looms large on the horizon at the end of the mid-morning break. Haydn hasn't bothered to complete the necessary crib-sheet, no doubt expecting to extort a document from one of us. But none of *us* had bothered either, as we confidently expected the test to be one of those straight-forward affairs with no awkward questions or complicated theorems to learn.

Sitting in the snug warmth of the library, we sympathise with Our Hero's plight. No crib sheet and no time to make one.

We scratch our heads and look skywards for a possible solution.

"What tha bahna do, Mitch? If tha dunt get seven arter ten, tha'll gerr a Sat'day."

"Charlie Spur'll chuck t'booard-rubber at thi if tha can't do it."

"If tha gets a Sat'day, tha weeant be able ter play for t'schooil."

"What tha bahna tell thi father if tha gets done?"

With each passing remark Our Hero becomes more and more desperate - he cannot/must not fail. But he hasn't done his homework; he hasn't learned the work; he can't remember anything. The spectre of a BGS-committed Saturday morning begins to loom ominously over the fast-approaching horizon.

Head in hands, he groans and contemplates his fate. But then a steely glint lights up his eye. The intelligence which got him to the Grammar school in the first place swings into gear and a hastily contrived, artful plan takes shape...

Scouting round the library, Haydn finds a vacant radiator - one of those massive old-fashioned types which is blasting out its quota of winter play-time heat. He draws up a leather-backed library chair and carefully positions himself facing the central-heating appliance, knees up against it. Leaning forward, he rests his forehead in one of the shoulders of the radiator and remains motionless for the rest of the break-time period.

After ten minutes or so, panic-alarm bells began to sound for the rest of us. Haydn's face has turned a deep-beetroot colour and he has begun to utter low moaning sounds towards the library floor.

"Ey up, Mitch. Are y'awreight? Tha's gone a funny colour."

"'Coorse Ah'm reight. Ah'm gerrin aht o' t'Maths test. Just leave me alone..."

The bell sounds for the end of our fifteen minutes' worth of welcome release from the classroom prison and we prepare to make our desolate way towards *that* Maths test.

"Sithee, Mitch. It's time ter gooa."

But Haydn has other ideas. He raises his forehead from the radiator to reveal cranial skin which has almost seared itself to the red-hot metal. With flushed face and an admirable shambling gait, Our Purple-Faced Hero makes his way towards the School Secretary's office, moaning and groaning and clutching his belly.

Wondering what on earth he is up to, the rest of us leave him to it and begin reciting theorems to each other in preparation for the impending test...

Haydn taps politely on Miss Laxton's door.

Our School Secretary, a clean-living and upright spinster in her late forties, answers the knock. She is shocked to encounter a half-crouching 3-Alpha boy in obvious distress.

She is treated to an Oscar-worthy performance of quality and precision.

Ah'm gerrin aht o' t'Maths test.
Just leave me alone..."

"Miss, Ah'm nooan ser well. Ah dooant feel reight at all," groans Haydn in the perfect *bona fide* imitation of a man at Death's Very Door.

"Oh, you poor boy," exclaims Miss Laxton in sincere concern for a pupil's welfare. "Let me look at you," and she places a tender hand on Mitch's forehead.

"Oh my goodness! You're running a temperature - feverish indeed. You must go and lie down in the Medical Room and I'll make you a hot drink..."

Haydn's "fever" lasted until precisely 12.00 mid-day. Shortly after we had sweated our way through Charlie Spurr's Maths Test, Our Hero joins us in the Dining Room, sits down for his dinner with the rest of us, and eats a hearty meal.

Meanwhile, back in the smoky atmosphere of the Staff Room, the teacher's mark book for the recent test is completed with the following entry:

Butler   F.A. $^5/_{10}$ (detention)
Mitchell   H.   Absent

***

MESSAGES

I belong to a generation of children who were forced to go to Sunday School, whether they liked it or not.

Up to the age of ten or eleven, in all the places I ever lived, every Sunday afternoon I was packed off in my best clothes for an hour or two's worth of Religious Instruction. If my Dad said that I had to go, then that was the end of the matter. Any protests would be summarily silenced with a sharp clout and off I'd traipse up the road to church, often in disgruntled disgust.

All the way there, I'd chunter and mumble to myself as I dragged my Sunday Best heels slowly and reluctantly along the pavement for the mile or so to our local place of worship. What made matters a whole lot worse was that I'd have to pass the end of Welland Close, where all my day-school mates would be hanging about, riding their bikes, firing their catapults or planning to rob their next telephone-box.

Crossing my fingers that they have decided to play somewhere else, I round the bend. But I'm out of luck. I flatten myself up against garden walls in an effort to blend in with the brickwork and sneak past unnoticed.

"Wheer tha offter, Freddie," Kenny Blacklock shouts across the road and my heart sinks.

"Ah'm offter see me auntie in 'Eckmondwike an' Ah maunt miss t'next bus," I lie, and attempt to run off.

Pongo Nixon calls after me as I race off in red-faced

embarrassment: "Tha wants ter come wi' us lot. We're offter t'buildin' site to start t'dumper up an' fill all t'tubs wi' water an' wang bricks through t'winders. Tha owt ter 'ear glass smashin'. It's real."

And all the way round the corner and out of sight, I envied them their Estate Kids' Sunday afternoon fun.

The most excitement *I* could expect during the next two hours or so was another attendance stamp for my Sunday School record book. This stamp would depict a biblical scene [in colour] and it would be meticulously stuck in place on the appropriate date-space, by our dog-collared vicar, the Reverend R.T. Merryweather. Upon return back home, suitably purified of sin and spiritually uplifted, the stamp in my book would prove to Mum and Dad that I'd been in attendance, so the idea of truanting with Kenny Blacklock and the Welland Close Boys was out of the question.

I'd make my reluctant way inside the Church Hall to be met by all the other "nice" kids in their Sunday best. We're all ready to soak up another session of holy information-gathering and hymn-singing.

Now, to a lad of nine or ten, I have to say that a lot of the subtle messages I was given at such sessions were a bit confusing, to say the least. Oh yes, of course they were all good tidings and sound moral values which have stood me in fine stead for the rest of my life. And each message/story brought its reward of the illustrated stamp for my attendance book. But they were full of baffling contradictions with which I've only recently come to terms. I can vividly remember asking a very important question one bright afternoon in spring, just after a long and tedious Sunday School address by the Reverend Merryweather. After a fairly long pause for contemplation of today's uplifting session, I am perplexed by the question which has been taxing my young brain for the past few minutes.

I whisper urgently to my pal Glynn Coggan: "Hey, Coggie. 'Ow come we get to 'ave *two* Dads?"

Coggie is similarly non-plussed. He shakes his head in like-bewilderment as we make our way out of the old wooden doors at the back of the Church Hall.

You see, the Reverend always stressed the point that Our Father in Heaven was always watching over us, but I knew, for a fact, that I'd just left my Dad back home, not thirty minutes ago, weeding in the back garden. So I wanted to know who this other bloke was who was always around us and who called himself "Our Father".

The one at home went out to work in the foundry five and half days a week, took me to football matches and bought me a sweetie surprise every Friday night. But the Other Fellow never showed up - ever. So in my young person's view of things, the Dad who lived with us was a much safer bet.

Thus confused, I proffered my attendance book at the end of the Sunday School session, accepted my coloured stamp and eagerly scrutinized it on the way home. I was searching for some pictorial evidence of the current week's teaching. But it was to no avail.

The brightly coloured image before me showed a bursting cloud of dazzling light in the sky. A little cherub-faced child looked up into the sky from below, his face aglow with a beaming smile. And that was all there was to that.

A few sessions later, my nipper's noddle has just about accommodated the idea of Our Father in Heaven, as well as the one who worked at P & C Garnett's, Textile Machine Makers, Cleckheaton. But then, the Reverend Merryweather delivers another message which throws a holy spanner deep into the spiritual workings of my tiny child's mind:

God is *three* people - all at the same time! There's God the Father, God the Son and God the Holy Ghost.

Now, this last one really puts the frighteners on me when I first hear about it.

I am given it on good authority that the Holy Ghost is watching over me all the time - wherever I go and whatever I am up to. At school, out playing down Land's Beck making dams, or at home in my bedroom, this person is always there, keeping a spiritual eye on me. But I can't actually see him, because he is a ghost, who sometimes goes by the name of the Holy Spirit.

As a result of all this, my nocturnal behaviour undergoes a dramatic modification the moment I enter my bedroom.

Upon hearing in detail about the Holy Ghost, every shadow in my bedroom after lights-out now takes on the threat of a presence in the room, looming over me and keeping watch. I dive under the covers on a nightly basis, cuddle up close to my hot-water bottle and daren't show my face again till dawn's early light filters through the curtains.

What with two dad's and the Holy Ghost for company every night, it's all a bit overwhelming for me.

It's not all bad news, however. According to the Reverend

the third member of the Holy Team - God the Son - turns out to be a Top Person.

Jesus of Nazareth is everybody's idea of a favourite Big Brother. He turns water into wine, feeds five thousand folk with five Mother's Pride and two pieces of haddock, *and* walks on water. So we are all in youthful awe of such a Magnificent Person, and we share in the Reverend Merryweather's joy at the very mention of His name.

But our confusion returns when we hear of His demise.

It appeared to us that all those Pharisees and Saducees didn't realise when they were on to a good thing. We couldn't for the life of us understand why they didn't like Jesus feeding all those folk and turning water into wine. And we were positively astounded when the rotten old Pharisees got one of His own side to betray Him - with a *kiss*!!!

We nudged each other and sniggered when we were first told about that little escapade.

In our view of things, blokes just did *not* kiss other blokes. We all eagerly examined our coloured stamps for *that* picture, but we were disappointed to discover that it was only an image of Our Lord being carted off by a gang of Roman soldiers.

For a month or two after we first heard that story, however, the Reverend Merryweather' credibility amongst us was at a very low ebb, I can tell you. And as if all the afore-mentioned confusing messages aren't enough to completely baffle us, the Reverend's next snippet of Sunday School information upsets us even more.

We'd just nicely begun to get over the fact that Our Lord had been betrayed by a kiss from one of His gang, when

Rev. Merryweather makes another astounding Sunday afternoon announcement.

He told us, in fine detail, that when the Romans had finally captured their quarry, they called in the Royal Air Force!

"... And then Jesus was taken before Pontius Pilate," he informed us, gravely and with much sadness one Sunday afternoon, just before he gave us that week's pictorial stamp for our attendance books.

Naturally, lads of our generation were all on the look-out for Spitfires, Wellington Bombers and RAF roundels in the pictures, but, as you might expect, we didn't find any aeronautical information whatsoever...

The following week, things got even worse.

The Reverend was almost in tears as he recounted that, after His brush with the RAF, Our Lord was tried, found guilty and nailed on the cross. I well remember how upset we all were at that idea, but can you imagine our youngsters' confusion when we are told that all this took place on *Good* Friday?

" 'Ow does he mean *Good* Friday," I whispered to Coggie, at the back of the Sunday School room. Utterly confused, I put the question: "What's ser *good* abaht 'avin ter be nailed on a cross by all them lousy Romans?"

"Dunno," replies Coggie. "An' Ah'll tell thi summat else..." He knits his brow.

"Ah can't understand why all t'buns at Easter are 'ot an' cross. Mebbe they wor upset abaht Our Lord evvin' all t'nails brayed through 'is 'ands..."

And we scrutinize our pictorial stamps in vain for any

kind of solutions to our confusing religious dilemmas. None are forthcoming.

After Easter, Rev. Merryweather is overjoyed as he communicates the most important message of the Church year. He beams and smiles throughout the entire afternoon Sunday School as he announces joyfully to his young charges: " ... and after conquering death, Our Lord ascended into Heaven ..."

We gratefully accept our stickers but, as we peruse the picture of Our Lord being uplifted skywards on a cloud, we are again somewhat puzzled.

"'Appens 'e's joined t'RAF wi' Pilot Pontius," observed Coggie.

Our confusion continues throughout the ecclesiastical year...

And, in the twinkling of a nostalgic childhood eye, we arrive at the most baffling time of the religious year - Christmas. For mind-boggling messages, this is Prime Confusion Time in any kiddie's life - and mine was no exception...

After frightening the living daylights out of me with their ideas about the Holy Ghost - who forever patrolled my night-times to keep a round-the-clock eye on me - the grown-ups in my childhood world introduced me to another Mysterious Nocturnal Presence.

The old chap in question sported a red dressing-gown, black, shiny boots and was completely unshaven. He maintained the aura of a spectre because he crept about my bedroom once a year in the wee small hours, after forcing an entry down the chimney. In addition to visiting me at the dead of night, however, he also managed to creep round every other kid's bedroom throughout the whole wide world.

This old chap, it seemed to me, was also a member of the Ecclesiastical Flying Club but *he* was the proud owner of an aeronautical transport vehicle pulled by flying reindeers. In giving him a slightly more human appearance, this made him just a wee bit more acceptable than the Holy Ghost, but only just.

Now how scary is that when you're only five or six and still very damp behind your hearing apparatus? But at least Santa Claus/Father Christmas left some decent gear in our bedrooms before he departed for twelve months to that magical land full of fairies and elves.

During these formative years of my life, every Christmas was celebrated with a family visit to my dad's homeland [and the county of my birth] - Stapleford, Notts.

Dad's sister - my Aunty Nelly - still lived in the Butler family home of eighty years or so - a two-up, two-down red-brick terraced house on Pasture Road. Built at the turn of the century, it still had its antiquated gas-lighting and a dark, cold outside toilet. And at Christmas, that little house filled up to bursting point.

As soon as my dad came home from P & C Garnett's for the Yuletide Holiday, we would all climb into our old black Vauxhall Velox - Mum and Dad in the front, brother Robin and I in the back - to make the annual pilgrimage from the Shoddy Towns to Nottinghamshire. The old Vauxhall would chug south at 30mph, through Sheffield centre, Norton Woodseats, Heanor and Ilkeston to arrive in plenty of time for Yuletide celebrations in Stapleford.

It was our Christmas joy to spend two or three fairly cramped, uncomfortable but happy nights at number 190, having evicted Aunty Nelly, Uncle Berrisford and Cousin Charles from their usual sleeping quarters. And now, to add to my childhood store of confused messages, what images of Christmas-past come flooding back!

I recall vividly the nightfall in the small back-room. As a real treat, I would be allowed to climb up onto that table where, the following day, the Christmas Turkey of Turkeys would be served up. Handed a lighted match by my dad, I am allowed to hook my chubby finger through the ring and to pull down on the slender chain to release a hiss of coal-gas.

Taking great care not to damage the fragile white mantle of the lamp, I hold the lighted match aloft and rejoice in the "pop" of the igniting gas. Snug and warm in the glowing white light, we all prepare for the annual Yuletide gathering of the Butler clan.

What to my child's mind, seems like a host of uncles, aunties and cousins arrive in the back room as the night wears on. Bathed in the gas-light from above, and comfortably enveloped in the aroma of mild bottled ale and sweet sherry, we crowd round the table, the youngsters sitting two to a seat. Out come the playing cards and it's time for some festive family fun.

Vast fortunes of pre-decimal coinage rapidly proceed to change hands during games of Pontoon and Newmarket. The uncles take turns at running the bank, the damage to wallet being no object at this festive time of year. Now and again, there is the glint of silver in the pile of halfpennies, pennies and threepenny bits.

"Ooh! Look 'ere," says my Dad every year of my childhood. "Somebody's playing with some snow..."

And inevitably, after the last round of Newmarket, with piles of cash still on the table, Dad reaches into his waistcoat pocket to extract the little brass top - "Put-and-Take". And every year, without fail he chortles gleefully: "Now then. Let's play Wotsitsname..."

I remember two different models of the inch-high brass spinning top, either of which would make its annual Yuletide appearance from Dad's waistcoat pocket, depending on his mood. If he fancied some top-drawer financial Yuletide fun, he would produce the Mark Two version. This one had a separate section just below the slender, knurled handle, which spun independently of the main body.

Each face of the body was etched with a number - 1 to 6. But the real damage was done with the afore-mentioned top section. On each of the faces was etched a set of figures. For the gambling fraternity, these were the odds - from "Evens" right up to "8-1".

So now, we're ready for some fun and Dad rubs his hands in gleeful Yuletide anticipation.

Each of the adults around the table is "invited" to be the bookie for a round of spins of the deadly top. In the Butler household, a refusal to accept such a post of responsibility is frowned upon, so there's no escape.

Having a great deal of experience in the field of top-spinning, Dad invests himself with the honorary position as Starter, and the Christmas Top whirls away on the polished table-top.

"...And it's number three," announces Mr Starter. "4-1, Berrisford. Get yer 'and in yer pocket..."

"Tuppence 'ere," demands young Michael Keetley. "Tuppence!" The second utterance more commanding and demanding than the first, which elicits a grimacing frown from Uncle Berrisford.

Chortles all round and, with a forced grin, Berrisford stumps up the ready cash from his back pocket.

The night wears on and more empty beer-bottles fill the kitchen shelf. Sherry glasses are replenished with zealous enthusiasm, and the stakes in the Yuletide Handicap begin to increase.

"Ooh, look 'ere," observes Mr Starter. "More snow!" And a few tanners* and bobs* appear in the pile of invested cash.

Around eleven o'clock, when that Old White-Haired Gentleman is well on his way, the aunties and females drop out of the race. The cash sums are far too high and already, there are signs of frayed tempers amongst the men.

"Well, that's a bogger," declares Mr Starter as the top lands on Number Two at odds of 8-1.

"One and sixpence," shrieks young Keetley in that demanding, commanding tone again. The steely flash of my Dad's eyes tells me that this particular successful punter is but a whisker away from a clout round the ear.

After the pay-out and to avoid unnecessary bloodshed, we youngsters are ushered off to bed...

* For those born after decimalisation, sixpences and shillings, in the days when five Woodbines cost ninepence

And so begins the Yuletide event that was the annual Christmas Eve adventure.

With neither gas-light nor toilet in the upper storey of Aunty Nelly's household, bed-time procedures were conducted by candle-light in Arctic conditions. Our heads are stuffed full of the images of spinning-tops, tuppences, Santa's sleigh and a host of reindeer, as younger brother and I make our scary way up the narrow staircase at the back of the living room.

Along the passage at the top, we follow Mum with her candle, fearful that, at any moment, she might disappear into the Christmas darkness ahead. We turn into our room, where dark, looming, shadows dance on the walls. Our beds await.

But that Christmas bedroom of long ago remains rooted in my memory for its introduction to the "guzunder".

In the biting winter chill of the bedroom and with teeth a-chatter, we don our pyjamas in a trice. To Hell with normal bedtime ablutions procedure, we think, save for the ritual emptying of the bladder. We grip the large rounded handles of that Yuletide chamber-pot in both hands and marvel at the clouds of dank vapour which rise into the Arctic air, high above our heads.

Full of hot, steaming liquid, the artefact is shoved deep into the dark recesses under the bed - filed carefully for future nocturnal use.

Many a time, I remember, I've shot out of bed with the urgent need of a child in the middle of the night, only to plant both feet up to the ankles into a carelessly filed chamber-pot full of pale, ice-cold, spent fluid...

And so it's time for the Night of Nights.

As the manly mumblings and mutterings and the merry clink of Yuletide silver from down below filter up the staircase, the candle is left to watch over our childhood's sleep.

Shadows dance and leap on the wall, and strange shapes appear at the window. Wierd ideas about the impending appearance of the Old Unshaven Chap in the Red Dressing-Gown become mixed up with the Holy Ghost's Patrol Duty and the Ecclesiastical Flying Club. I bury my way further down into the comforting, blanketed safety of the bed.

Thoughts of what will be at its foot the following morning soothe my fearful brow as the shadows from the flickering candle loom larger and larger. I finally drift away, fingers and toes tightly crossed that the Old Unshaven Chap will bring that Hornby "00" gauge clockwork train that I wrote to him about ...

But now, I have put off such childish thoughts. Older and much wiser, I take to my Yuletide bed this current Christmas Eve, and fifty-odd years have slipped across the skies on the sleigh of memories.

All those confused messages of long ago are still buzzing about in my brain-box and I must confess, I am still uneasy about the dead of night darkness in my bedroom. Was that Santa shuffling over there in the shadows by the wardrobe? Or was it the Holy Ghost, just calling in for a nocturnal check?

I burrow further down into the comforting safety of my bed and fall to pondering, like you do, to while away the sleepless hours...

As a kid, I was baffled by all the confusing messages. As a man, I remain confused. But one thing I do know: If we'd all given Our Lord a fair hearing first time round, then perhaps today, the world might have been a much different place.

Beneath the sheets, I shake my wise old head ruefully at the prospect of Lost Opportunities. But then, in a moment of silliness:

"...and perhaps those Easter buns wouldn't have been so hot and cross."

***

LIVING WITH THE TRUTH

When I was a lad, *nobody* told lies. That's because *all* the adults in my cosy little Shoddy Town world spun you the same line on the subject of "The Truth". They were unanimous as they presented a united front on the theme of deception, so in your oblivious childhood, you just took it all as gospel: "You must never, *ever* tell a lie."

If you ever gave in to the temptation to do a bit of fibbing, then the consequences were dire.

Top of the list was the Threat. Tell just *one* tiny fib and it was a Mortal Sin. As a direct result, you'd be in for a spot of eternal damnation on the Other Side when you finally got to meet your Maker.

You'd have to stand respectfully in front of The Pearly Gates, wait for St Peter to open the great leather-bound Book of Life and scan the list for your name.

If you were marked down in the "Mendacity" column as a *Liar, Dissembler, Fibber* or *Porky-Teller*, then it was back down the Golden Stairway for you, pal - a prime candidate for the *Other* [very warm] Place. Thus, throughout our childhood, like many other Shoddy Town kiddies, my brother and I lived in fear of telling a lie. We shared a healthy respect for the Truth and a common esteem for that Golden Stairway. So far, so good, you think.

All the little kids grow up completely pure, free from sin and never *ever* tell a lie. All the adults *know* that the kids will *always* tell them the Truth out of fear for the celestial consequences.

But there was a huge problem with such a philosophy that I vividly remember discovering one Friday tea- time in my dungareed infancy at about the age of four...

It had been a beautiful summer's day and I'd spent most of it out in the garden, playing with water in my little tin wheel-barrow. Every time my Mum used the tap inside, I would grab my little tin bucket and hold it under the kitchen drain-pipe in order to collect fresh supplies. Topping up my barrow, I circulated the garden, dispensing liquid refreshment to all the flowers in my Dad's quite extensive garden.

Now, my Dad, like so many working men of his generation, was a very keen gardener.

All his flower beds were meticulously tended, weeded and watered during his time-out from the foundry where he worked in the blasted heat of molten metal all day. Come finishing time and the five o'clock buzzer, he would dash home for his tea. As soon as it was devoured, he'd make like a rat from a trap for the greenhouse or the flower-beds. There he would potter about until dusk and The Last Post.

During the planting season, he spent hour after hour carefully arranging the tender young seedlings for the coming summer's colourful display. And come blossom-time, those plants would display their floral beauty in neat, regimented, soldier-like rows: ruby red tulips in single file; rank upon rank of golden marigolds; column after column of purple pansies.

But Dad's pride and joy were his Michaelmas Daisies.

They clung in tight rows to the edges of the sectioned

lawns of our modest semi-detached house, smiling and winking a yellow and mauve greeting to all who passed and paused to admire. At the height of the season, they were a border-edge of pure colour which left passers-by aghast at their splendour.

"Why, Mr Butler! What beautiful borders!" observe the old couple out on their evening stroll. "Such pretty colours! A picture! A wonderful sight!"

My Dad rises from his weeding position and politely raises his trilby. "Good evening. Pleasant now, isn't it?"

Hands on hips, he gazes fondly at his colourful charges round the edge of the lawn. Puffing out a proud horticultural chest: "Oh yes, my word. I grew them from seed, myself," he beams, and the old couple murmur their approval before strolling off...

Now, at the tender age of four, I have yet to develop my Dad's enthusiasm and devotion to gardening.

Not having yet cottoned on to the fact that much time, effort and money have been invested in the cultivation of the said Michaelmas Daisies, I regard them as mere playthings. They provide me with hours of endless arithmetical fun counting their many heads as I gently pull them off. Better still, their multi-coloured blossoms make pretty star-patterns against the green, close-cropped sward of the lawn, as they are plucked off and so arranged.

And after that, those spent heads are added to my bucket of water to create a thick, daisy soup...

An afternoon of high summer passes during which I innocently indulge in all of the afore-mentioned activities. As my earnest endeavours proceed, the lush green of the lawn becomes littered with a flush of Michaelmas Daisy colours. The borders, which were their erstwhile home, are green and bare, and a thick mixture of Michaelmas custard lines my little tin bucket, slopping over into the bottom of my little wheelbarrow.

The clarion call from my Mum in the kitchen heralds the approach of tea-time and informs me succinctly that play-time activities must cease forthwith. At the announcement of impending belly-filling activity, I am very pleased. My play-site is cleared in a flash, the contents of my tin bucket are dispensed down a drain and my wheelbarrow is parked up behind the garden shed. The evening routine begins...

Dad returns from the foundry. We take our evening meal and, after a suitable intermission for the smoking of one Player's Medium cigarette, he makes his customary way out into the garden.

In a few moments, he's back, ashen-faced, filling the air with foundryman's invective.

Many questions are forthcoming because he has discovered, amongst other things, tiny footprints on the lawn-edge, very close to the once-colourful Michaelmas Daisy border. In addition, the kitchen drain is blocked by an oozing, yellowish putrescence of Michaelmas custard.

And at this point in my childhood, I make an astounding discovery about "the Truth".

Having been educated in my early years to the idea that always telling the truth was a virtue, I was quite unprepared for the pay-off in doing so.

My Dad looms above me. The evening shadow of his

trilby-brim falls ominously across my upturned face as I prepare for bed. I fiddle nervously with the buttons on my pyjamas and look wide-eyed into my Dad's enraged eyes.

With a thunderous glare, I am interrogated in my night attire: "Did you pull the heads off those flowers, Freddie Butler? Now, tell me the truth - did you, eh?" And he leans forward to within a couple of inches of my now averted gaze.

Of course, I had to tell the truth, hadn't I? All that talk of the Celestial Stairway and St Peter had done its effective job and I come out with it, George Washington style. In the four year old's equivalent of "Yes, father it was me; I cannot tell a lie," I admit the lot and make a full and frank confession.

And then comes the bewildering pay off.

For coughing up the exact and honest truth, I am expecting to be praised, lauded and carried round the living-room shoulder high for being a Good Boy. But this is far from the case as I am subjected to a serious physical attack about my person, and I get the living daylights beaten out of me! I am whacked and clouted all over my puny four year-old body, while Dad rants and raves about respect for other people's property. Round and round we go, successive clouts raising ever-louder yelps of infant pain.

In an interesting variant to a straight-forward thrashing, I am beaten on the bum in rhythm as the admonishment continues up the little wooden staircase to bed:

And if - WHACK! Ever - WHACK!
You do it again - WHACK! WHACK!
I'll cut - WHACK! You - WHACK!
In two - WHACK! WHACK!

Finally, with a glowing-red arse to light my way, I am thrust into bed - and not allowed out until the following morning. Sobbing uncontrollably under the covers of my little wooden bed, I am very perplexed.

I have just been a very good boy and I've told the exact truth about my afternoon's horticultural activities. I've withheld nothing - not a single fact - and I've given my version of events as accurately as I possibly can, in the finest, minutest detail. But the reward has been a very severe thrashing and no bedtime cocoa.

So that night, in the dark beneath my infant bed-covers, I wipe away my tears, nurse a very sore bum and pass an internal memo to myself: In matters of the Truth, from this point onwards, I must become more selective.

If being truthful means a severe bashing about my body, then count me out, and to blazes with St Peter and his Book. But if it means that everybody smiles at me as they pat me on the head and praises my honesty, then that'll do for me. But it would all depend on a very swift risk assessment of the circumstances at the time.

On future occasions, before making any kind of statement, I resolve that a rapid appraisal of the consequences of telling the truth must be undertaken before an utterance of any kind passes my lips. And that's the way it stayed until events took a rather unexpected turn in July, 1949...

At this point in my life, I become a brother.

I well remember my Mum arriving home one summer's evening with a white bundle containing a pale, shrivelled prune with arms and legs. She informed me that this was "our Robin".

Shrugging my shoulders and heading off to the back-garden to continue my water-play with bucket and barrow, I passed a critical five-year old's observation: " 'E's a bit little for a brother, in't 'e?"

And life continued apace, but as we grew up, our Robin and I formed a lasting partnership in the Telling-the-Truth department. As he matures, we develop between us an enviable skill and adroitness in Risk Assessment procedures.

By the time he is six, we are able, in a matter of seconds and in a variety of circumstances, to arrive at Safety Precaution Policy Decisions. And in one matter in particular, we were successful for at least 15 years...

It was the summer of 1958 and I'd lately taken up residence in the second year at Batley Grammar School. A tidal wave of new educational information was engulfing me as the world of academia began to influence my life. Begowned and very learned masters were doing their utmost to ram vital, exam-passing information into my twelve year-old noddle, and, I must admit, I was beginning to soak it up. Most of it was new and exciting, capturing my 1950's naïve attention.

My most vivid recollection of it all, and one which has a direct bearing on the Telling the Truth theme, occurred one fine Spring day in the Science Laboratory.

Mr Lewis, our white-smocked, bespectacled Chemistry teacher is demonstrating the process of making chlorine. On the demonstration bench in front of us, there is a bewildering arrangement of conical flasks, bunsen burners, Kipps apparatus and glass bell-jars. "Screwy Lewie" is in full flow at the height of his demonstration when there is an unexpected lull in production of the acrid-smelling gas. Flasks cease to gurgle, vapours halt their copious flow, and the whole process grinds to a disappointing halt.

A thick silence descends on the captive audience as we wait expectantly for the gas-making process to re-start. One or two of the more daring boys begin to fidget on their stools and to whisper furtively to each other. In an attempt to stave off the swelling tide of potential disruption, Screwy informs us, by the by, that chlorine is the main constituent of household bleach.

"And what does Mother use bleach for, boys, eh?" he enquires, expecting an immediate response. But this is 1958 and a woman's place is still in the home. We men could hardly be expected to know the answer to such a searching domestic question. Blank looks all round, so Sir proceeds to demonstrate.

"Well, you see, Mum uses it to whiten the washing. And I shall now provide you with the living proof..."

He takes some bleach and a piece of old navy-blue cloth. Like a magician at Batley Variety Club, he waves his hands in the air and with a flourish, picks up a conical flask complete with cork stopper.

"And now, observe..." he hisses dramatically. At the same time, he uncorks the flask and pours some of the evil-smelling liquid onto the selected material.

We crane forward on our wooden laboratory stools, eager to observe the effects on the navy-blue of the cloth. For a while, nothing happens, but then, after a minute or two, a faint lightening cloud appears on the cloth. In about eight or nine minutes, during which we remain mesmerised, the cloud grows whiter and whiter, *before our very eyes*, and we are suitably gob-struck.

Shortly afterwards, gas-production resumes and the threat of potential disruption has been overcome.

I return home that evening, still mesmerised by the world-shattering revelations about the properties of bleach.

"Oh," I say to my brother, sitting on the end of my bed, prior to commencing the ritual of pre-tea-time homework. "Ah'll tell thi summat, nar..."

Our Robin is at junior school and still very impressionable about the academic world of study-at-home, exercise-books and logarithmic tables. He gazes in awe as I tip out my "Oxford" set of mathematical instruments, my "Collins" French dictionary and an assortment of pens, rulers and exercise books onto the drop-leaf table beneath my bedroom window.

"Dusta know what Ah've learned terday at schooil?"

This is a daft question, because I'm about to tell him anyway, and I proceed to outline the properties of bleach. I recount vividly and very accurately [with a few feet added for effect] the astounding incident of the navy-blue cloth.

"An' it went white as snow while we was watchin' it. Tha wouldn't a' believed it. Afore our very eyes," I concluded.

Despite his tender years, Robin was unimpressed.

In his seven year old equivalent of "Come, come, dearest brother! You're attempting to deceive me with a good-natured hoax," he invited me to prove my proposition/theory by reference to some bleach in a bottle beneath our kitchen sink. And he shot downstairs to get it.

After a furtive flit up and down the stairs, he returns with a large plastic bottle of "Household Bleach".

"Reight," he says, scornfully. "Let's see what yer talkin' abaht nar..."

We cast round our bedroom for a brightly coloured piece of material upon which to experiment. Items of clothing are examined and rejected; the floral bedroom curtains are too light in colour; the bedspreads are white anyway. Finally, we decide on the mauve coloured carpet which is next to my bed.

"So what tha does is this...," I state authoritatively, and I unscrew the cap from the bottle of potent liquid. Echoing the educational language of that morning, I announce: "And now, observe..." and I pour a small amount of the acrid-smelling liquid onto the carpet.

We wait, expectantly, for a slight initial blanching on our selected patch of carpet. For fully five minutes we watch that spot, kneeling beside it, noses to the floor, in eager anticipation.

After a couple of minutes, there is no change whatsoever in the colour of the carpet and Robin becomes increasingly scornful.

"What dusta mean *Afore your very eyes*," he chides. "Tha'r talkin' bollocks, our Freddie. Look at t'carpet - there's nowt up wi' it." And he pointed a stubby, derisory finger at the spot where the bleach had been poured.

I am perplexed. " 'Appens we 'aven't gi'n it enough," I state knowingly, and give the carpet a further, far more liberal, dose of the bleach.

A few more minutes pass and there is no change in the

colour of my bedroom floor-covering. Disappointed, we abandon it as a failed experiment and make our way downstairs for tea...

Later that evening, I return to our bedroom, dismally prepared for an hour of academic struggle to complete my Maths homework. I take my seat at the drop-down table, place my books on the table-top and reach down to my satchel for my Log Tables.

And it smacks me, right between the eyes. It shouts its presence from the roof-tops for all to see: a large sickly yellow patch, the size of a tea-towel, where once there had flourished the deep mauve of our bedroom carpet!

I gulp desperately as a wave of panic strikes. Decisive, evasive measures must be taken as of now, if not sooner. In frantic consultation with Our Robin, I devise an immediate response to the action of the bleach.

After obsequiously obtaining Mum's permission, "Just for a change, Mum, please..." , we effect an immediate, wholesale swap-round of our bedroom furniture.

We're into the bedroom like Pickford's Removal Men on drugs. In order to cover the offending area, chairs are re-positioned in seconds, wardrobes and beds shifted in minutes and after a quarter of an hour, the desired effect has been achieved. That sickly pale patch is well and truly out of sight, hidden away in the dark recesses below my bed.

And that's where it stayed - for the next fifteen years.

Nestling safely out of sight and out of mind, that pale yellow stain occupied the darkness of those nether regions throughout the entire length of my grammar school life. It even lay there, quiet, snug and saying nothing, all the way through my three-year teacher-training sojourn in the Capital. All that time, it kept shtumm, remained hidden away and was the very model of good behaviour.

Upon my return home, in 1966, it was there to welcome me, still pale yellow and still out of sight under my bed, a silent witness to my youthful experiment.

It accompanied me through the first two years of my teaching career at Batley High School and it maintained 100% attendance as I began to carve out my educational career at Earlsheaton School. Until February 1970, when the damned thing decided to poke its nose out after all those years of exemplary behaviour...

It was time for me to leave home - at Easter, 1970 - and to enter the marital stakes. Change was afoot at our house, since my leaving would free up some living space and this presented the opportunity for some chattel adjustment - particularly in the bedroom department.

One cold and dismal Sunday afternoon in February, with a growing sense of unease, I agreed to assist Our Robin and my Dad to move some bedroom furniture. We Butler offspring knew what was coming.

As my bed is lifted and carried out, my Dad, hands on hips exclaims; "What's goin' on 'ere..." as he makes the discovery. He gets down on his knees and peers closely at the fifteen year old patch on the carpet.

"What the bloody 'ell is all this," he asks incredulously, looking up at his two six-foot sons. "Who the bloody 'ell's med this mess???"

I looked at Our Robin and he returned my gaze. Years of practice told us that it was time for evasive action. All those childhood questions which we thought we'd seen the back of a few years ago, were on the point of re-surfacing.

The Family Inquisition was revving up for the re-convening process and all the old threats were about to be trotted out.

Like Pavlovian Dogs, Robin and I enter mental Risk Assessment Phase. Recalled visions of a sound rhythmical thrashing, being sent to bed with no supper and a refusal of passage through the Pearly Gates dominate my thinking.

Any second now, I expect to be given that parental grilling of yester-year: "Did you make that stain on the carpet, Freddie Butler? Now, tell me the truth - did you, eh?"

In the well-practised technique of buying-time, we shake our heads, stroke our chins and scratch the back of our heads whilst earnestly looking down at the sickly yellow stain.

After a suitable pause for invention, we trot out a selection of reasons for the carpet's variegated hue, plucked from the ether of our imaginations.

"It's faded - must 'ave bin t'sunlight."

"Poor quality carpet. Where did yer buy it from?"

"Must be a mark in t'pile where t'dog's wee'd on it..."

"It might be one o' Santa's footprints..."

"Or Rudolph's. It's gorran 'orse-shoe shape to it, 'ann't it?"

"Probably a fault in t'weave..."

And in his old age, Dad shakes his baffled old head, consigns the stain to the "One of Life's Mysteries" file and concludes the affair with his customary summing up: "Well, that's a bogger..."

We two heave a sigh of relief. No thrashing, no bedroom confinement. We got away with it and the Truth remains buried for ever. Or does it?

A repeated, returning vision haunts me as I plod through the rest of my life, on my way to St Peter and the Pearly Gates. I would like to think that my passage through them is guaranteed; no problem; all in order. But I have one or two nagging doubts...

My Shoddy Town life is done and I begin to mount the Golden Stairway. Raising an aged head, I look up.

At the top, in a dazzling burst of celestial light, the golden-robed figure awaits. His long, flaxen hair matches the hue of his beard which reaches down to the sparkle of his jewelled belt, hung from which is a huge golden key. In the crook of his robed arm, he holds the great leather-bound Book of Life.

It is open at the page for surnames beginning with "B".

Behind him, bathed in glorious sunlight, are the huge, Pearly Gates, awesome in their golden splendour. They are closed.

I reach the top step and St Peter smiles a welcoming celestial smile. He looks down at the Book. But the beam of his visage soon darkens and turns to a frown of consternation as he runs a holy finger down the lists of names.

"Ah, now who have we here...Ah yes, Butler F.A."

After a brief scrutiny of the entry opposite my name, St

Peter the Gatekeeper fixes me right between the eyes with a pointed, divine stare. "Weren't you responsible for some ruined floor-covering in July 1958?"

"Well, you see, sir..." I begin, entering Risk Assessment Phase, desperately trying to buy some celestial time. "Er... um... it was probably a fault in the weave..."

* * *

"Weren't you responsible for some ruined floor-covering in July, 1958?"

AND THINGS  THAT GO BUMP...

Ever since I can remember, I've always been frightened of the dark.

A perfectly friendly, cosy room by day becomes a haunted, evil den of ghosts, ghouls and spirits as soon as the curtains are drawn and the lights go out. Windows rattle, doors creak, the dead-of-night wind moans round the eaves of the house, and I am a quivering mass of terrified human jelly. I dive for cover under any friendly blanket or behind any benign settee which happens to be near. And there I remain, until dawn's early light.

And I think I've discovered the reason why...

When I was really small, at the age of about 3 or 4, my Dad discovered a very successful method of instant discipline for control of his first born son, such an honour having been bestowed upon Yours Truly. This method, I am told, never failed to exercise due care and control of a naughty, tantrum throwing infant. It proved to be entirely successful during the early years of my life and I was, apparently, the very model of a well-behaved fledgling. Such a purposeful and successful disciplinary effect was achieved by reference to an elfin being who went by the name of Johnny Goblin.

But this Johnny Goblin was no mythical being who never showed any earthly form. Quite the opposite, in fact. He lived and thrived, along with many other items of domestic table-wear, in the cupboard at Aunty Nelly's house in Stapleford, Notts. His dwelling-place was in the dark recesses of that living-room corner-cupboard - on top of a cream-coloured tea-pot!

Now before you throw this book down in abject disgust, avowing that the author has lost what few marbles he had, please allow me to explain...

Good old Aunty Nelly, as already recounted, lived in a red-brick terrace-house in the depths of Nottinghamshire, and it was our good fortune to visit her and my Uncle Berrisford every now and then. But at the time I'm talking about, my grandfather, Arthur Butler, was still a member of that household. So a trip to Stapleford was akin to a Gathering of the Clans in the Butler family.

On such visits, *my* Dad [F.A.Butler Senior] was on his mettle as a parent, always anxious to indicate to *his* Dad [Arthur] what an efficient father his son had turned out to be.

Even when I knew him, Arthur was a very straight-laced Victorian gentleman with a sombre and forbidding presence and a grey moustache. In a curious tweak of ironic coincidence, he had been in service towards the end of the nineteenth century as a butler to the Viceroy of Ireland and he had "buttled" in the strict regime of that upper class establishment for the Prince of Wales in Dublin. So in Arthur's presence, everybody had to be on their meticulously best behaviour.

He dominated his family with the proverbial rod of iron, ruling the roost and brooking no nonsense whatsoever at any time. Everything had to be in the strictest apple-pie order and every domestic event had to take place at the correctly appointed hour. An upbringing in such a household probably accounted for *my* Dad's slavish adherence to "routine". You know the sort of thing: Breakfast at eight in the morning; "dinner" at 12 noon; tea at 5 o'clock; bed at 10.30...

And there's another day gone!

I used to secretly admire my Dad's internal biological alarm-clock which would tell him exactly what time it was, no matter where he happened to be on Planet Earth: Ten to breakfast; Half past mi dinner; Quarter to tea-time.

Come any given meal-time, Dad would be sitting up to the table, knife and fork at the ready, salivating in expectant Pavlovian fashion at precisely the appointed hour...

Of course, in later life, my brother and I used to laugh at him, marvelling at the fact that my Mum readily complied with the regularity of his alimentary time-piece. At twelve noon, "dinner" was *always* on the table at the first precise chime of Dad's internal Big Ben, just as his knife and fork were entering descent mode.

Breakfast was already laid up ready the night previous, and 5 o'clock tea-time would find the three of us men all round the table at precisely the moment our mashed potatoes hit the plate. And that's how it was for fifty five years of Mum and Dad's wedded bliss...

But at the time I'm talking about, in the late 1940's, my Dad had returned to his family home for a visit, and I was to be used as living proof of his parenting skills. All of which brings us back to Johnny Goblin.

Sitting on top of the cream coloured tea-pot with a mischievous, leering grin on his elfin face, J.G. was the green and red tea-pot lid handle. Confined to the dark depths of Aunty Nelly's cupboard for the greater part of the year, he only came out when visitors arrived for a cup of tea. On such an occasion, he made his entry into my life.

"See 'im, there," hissed my Dad to me, one bright Sunday afternoon in 1948, just after we'd finished an afternoon tea of tinned-salmon sarnies and cherry-topped buns. " 'E's called Johnny Goblin, an' if you're a naughty boy, 'e comes at night to get yer." He pointed meaningfully at the tea-pot figurine.

Turning away, he winked knowingly at all the adults in the room, including Grandad Arthur.

The grown-ups chuckle secretively as they notice my child's eyes widen in fearful wonder. Swallowing hard, I ask incredulously: "What does 'e do?

" 'E creeps under yer bed, an' 'e pokes yer. An' if yer a very bad lad, 'e fetches all the other goblins to hide under yer bed an' give yer a poke, too," says Dad, warming to his task now, whilst receiving nods of approval from Arthur.

"Oh, an' if yer a *really* bad lad, 'e teks away all yer presents 'at Santa's brought, " he adds as an after-thought.

"But if yer a good boy, an' y'always eat the fat off yer bacon, 'e'll stay on top o' that tea-pot in that cupboard, an' e'll never bother yer - *ever*," was Dad's summing up of the situation.

By now, I am convinced that my child's world is under constant surveillance by Johnny Goblin and his gang of nasty little henchmen. Wherever I go, whatever I do, J.G. and his chums are there - in my bedroom behind night-time curtains, lurking in the deep recesses at the back of my toy-drawer or even heavily camouflaged behind the lavatory-pan. They lurk in dark corners, waiting to pounce if I do anything naughty.

As a result, parental discipline is instant. Whenever I am instructed to do anything at which I might baulk, the merest hint of J.G's impending arrival and I comply willingly, trembling in body-wracking terror.

Having thus demonstrated successfully to Arthur such refined and effective parenting skills, Dad is happy. I slowly go on growing up, the very model of a well-behaved infant - Seen and not Heard

On future visits to our ancestral home, it becomes one of my Dad's party tricks to demonstrate the effectiveness of his Infant Behaviour-Modification Technique. It was always good for a few laughs with any Nottingham-based members of the family who happened to be around...

A knowing wink to the adults, a surreptitious, secretive rattle of a door handle anywhere in the house accompanied by a shout of " 'E's 'ere! It's Johnny Goblin! 'E's come down off that tea-pot!"   The effect on me is instant.

In a frenzy of infant dread, I dash like a hounded jack-rabbit desperate for a bolt-hole. Under a settee; into a corner behind the 12-inch television; onto a window-sill in the folds of a curtain; I dash anywhere to avoid the groping, poking fingers of J.G.

Whilst I wet myself in trembling fear, the adults almost wet themselves laughing at my terror-stricken plight. And they continue to laugh long after Dad goes to the cupboard door, peers in and announces Johnny's return to his station on top of the tea-pot, for the time being, at any rate.

I creep out cautiously, my Christmas presents assured

until the next time J.G. climbs down off the tea-pot lid and shows his green and red, gnarled little face...

Perhaps such parental input was responsible for my dread of Santa, too.

At the time when all other kids were eagerly anticipating the arrival of the white-haired Old Gentleman in the Red Suit, I lived in trouser-filling terror.

From about the beginning of December, our infant class was throbbing with talk of Nativity Plays, the Three Wise Men and the impending visit to Santa's grotto in town. Play-time talk was dominated by discussions about how The Old Gentleman in Red managed to get down a two-foot square hole and out into your house - wandering about in there at the dead of night.

Such talk did nothing to reassure me, and I would spend a month or so diving beneath the sheets each bedtime and not surfacing until morning.

Any noise of wind moaning round the eaves, the stifled bark of next-door's dog or even the flushing of a late-night toilet would have me trembling in anticipatory anguish. I would worm my way as far down the bed as was humanly possible without suffocating. Down there, cocooned in the comforting darkness, I would hold an infant conversation with myself:

"That must 'ave been 'Im," I would whisper hoarsely to myself. " 'E's come already an' left me nowt..."

But imagine, if you will, the trepidation with which the following parental anouncement is received when it's delivered round our tea-table, about a week before Christmas:

"...And this week-end, we're off ter see Santa in 'is grotto."

All the grottoes I'd read about were full of elves and fairies who helped Santa on his Yuletide nocturnal excursions. For all I knew, *Johnny Goblin might be with them*. Him and his chums, waiting round the corner of the dim passage-way at Woolworth's store, or lurking behind the fairy-lit Christmas Tree.

But if F.A.Butler [Senior] said we were going to see Santa, then so be it...

The following Saturday afternoon we stand at the bus-stop, ready for our Yuletide excursion to Lapland. When it hoves to, and to Mum and Dad's intense embarrassment, I have to be dragged onto the bus, squirming and trembling in my childish reluctance to travel to town.

In similar mode, I am dragged off again in the town-centre.

We walk round the shops, taking in the festive atmosphere of twinkling lights, barrel-organ music and joyful Saturday afternoon laughter. Throughout our stroll, I devise a variety of infantile ploys in the effort to stave off the inevitable consultation with the Old Gentleman in Red.

I lose my cap in Boots the Chemist's; I have to stop at regular intervals to fasten my trouser buttons; I desperately need to go to the toilet. But all such ploys are utterly unsuccessful and eventually we arrive outside Woollies, primed and ready for the visit.

Santa's grotto is in the far corner of the store, bathed in a pool of colour from the fairy lights round its entrance.

I peep round my Dad's trouser leg and take in the scene. I notice the dark chasm beyond the life-size picture of

Rudolph with his glowing hooter. I see other kids and their parents paying their dues to the life-size gnarled old gnome at the entrance before they make their excited ways out of sight round the dark bend in the passage.

By the time the Butler family are at the head of the queue, the Johnny Goblin factor has taken over. My bottom lip trembles as the green-and-red suited Old Gnome takes our fare for the trip.

" 'E's wearin' a Johnny Goblin uniform. 'E's one of 'em," I exclaim to myself.

I yank at my Dad's overcoat tails in a forlorn indication that I would rather forego the next few minutes' worth of Yuletide fun.

But Dad is having none of it."Come along, now, Our Freddie. We're off ter see Santa," he states firmly.

In a fit of terror I turn tail to flee, but my Dad's vice-like grip fastens round my thigh as he whisks me aloft, under his arm. Red-faced with embarrassment now, smiling sheepishly at a queueful of cheerfully expectant parents and beaming kiddies, he drags me off down the passage into the dimly lit depths of the grotto.

We round a corner and there, sitting on a log, muttering and mumbling, is the White-haired Old Gentleman in Red who I am convinced has already been stalking the dark recesses of my bedroom only a couple of nights ago.

"I've brought Our Freddie ter see yer, Santa," chortles Dad, nodding and winking knowingly.

Santa greets us with outstretched arms. "Well, then, Freddie. Ho! Ho! Ho! Come and sit on Santa's knee an' tell him what yer want for Christmas."

In an internal, infantile version of "Not f...... likely," I let out with a scream of terror and desperately fight my way over Dad's shoulder:

"Don't want 'im! Don't like 'im!"

Dad has all on to claw me back from the roof of the grotto as I desperately attempt to flee. His profuse apologies to Santa echo down the years as we depart back up the tunnel, and another Yuletide visit passes into oblivion...

And so I go on growing up, frightened of the dark.

As each twilight of my childhood descends, every sunset brings the menacing promise of Johnny Goblin, the White-Haired Old Gentleman in Red, both accompanied by an evil army of below-the-bed gnomes and nasty little elves...

Now, as you well know, darkness is a definite pre-requisite when viewing films of any kind, so cinemas and the Hollywood merry-go-round of the fifties and sixties continue to stoke my fear throughout my spotty youth.

On any Saturday night, in the foyer of the Essoldo or The Playhouse down Dewsbury, I quake in fear. The lass I have just met outside the Bon Bon cafe was late, so we'll have to enter our chosen picture palace after the start of the programme. This will mean a journey down the side-aisles in darkness, led by the pencil-beam of the usherette's torch.

A trip in the dark! The sweat breaks out on my brow and I shake in terror at the thought. The spectre of Johnny Goblin lurks behind every cinema-seat as my escort and I make our ways to our seats. We arrive at our destination and I am a quivering mass of uncontrollable adolescent terror.

"Don't want 'im! Don't like 'im!"

It doesn't take me long to figure out why it is that a succession of pretty young things from the Girls' Grammar School soon lose interest in accompanying a whimpering coward for two bob's worth of Saturday night darkness.

I spend the greater part of my adolescence trying to conquer my fear...

So, given all the afore-mentioned statistics, you'd think that someone with my particular aversion to the night-time dark would avoid such lack-of-light situations in later life, wouldn't you? Now that I am grown up and sensible, it would be wise to stick to daylight activities at all times, wouldn't it? Not so, because the worst is yet to come!

It's 1972 and at the rapidly advancing age of twenty-eight, at Earlsheaton School in Dewsbury, one dark and lonely night, I encountered the School Ghost - in the School Hall, in the School Darkness...

By now, I've tucked nine happy years of teaching under my educational belt. Keen, eager and full of enthusiasm to promote extra-curricular activities amongst the pupils, I readily enter into any after- school schemes and ideas. One such was my own invention - a Film Club.

Enthusiastically promoted with an entrance hall notice board and assembly announcements, the Film Club became, at the height of its success, quite a well-supported activity, despite its rather intellectual-sounding title. But we weren't particularly interested in the so-called "arty" films of the time. Not for us the in-depth discussions about characterisation in "Richard the Third" or the tension generated in "Citizen Kane". Oh no.

What we wanted was to give as many kids as possible a good entertaining time, with rip-roaring action and pop and crisps on sale at the interval.

Films like "The Great Escape", "Villa Rides" and "Where Eagles Dare" were good crowd-pullers on Thursday evenings at 10p per head and they could be easily hired for "shut-in" locations at reasonable rates.

The School Hall was well set up to show films of this nature.

There was, and still is, a projection room, a large screen and an auditorium which would hold at least three hundred paying customers. But, as with most educational initiatives of the time, there was a bit of a problem...

On the evenings in question, the caretaker was unavailable to open/lock up the premises. Other pressing responsibilities demanded his time and attendance at the Spangled Bull in Earlsheaton. So, if the Film Club was to thrive, then the security job would have to be undertaken by Yours Truly.

Arriving in Caretaker Mode at about 7.00pm for a 7.30pm kick-off, I open up the main door of the school.

Switching smoothly and efficiently into Projectionist Mode, I set up the 16mm film projector and erect the big silver screen on the stage. Then I sit back and await the arrival of the hordes.

A few minutes later the audience filters in through the big glass doors of the entrance hall. They are met by the Usherette [me].

I relieve them of their 10p entrance fees and show them to their seats. As the doors close, I dash upstairs to re-assume the Projectionist's responsibilties. Lights Out and cue Reel One!

After about two hours' worth of on-screen fighting and fun, the show finishes. The credits slide across the silver screen and the kids leave in a high state of excitement.

All the way down Bywell Road, Syke Lane and Chickenley Lane there would be noisy re-enactments of various acts of bravado witnessed that night in the darkness of the school hall.

Down a gloomy Bywell Road, Steve McQueen would be roaring alongside that barbed-wire prison fence on his motor-bike. Or Charles Bronson would once again line up five or six Mexican peasants, one behind the other, and shoot them all with one bullet. And Clint Eastwood would perhaps be re-climbing the slender wire of that cable car.

Back in the now-silent school, I was left to re-wind the reels, pack up the equipment and lock up the premises. If I got on with the job, I might make last orders in The Whistler for a relaxing, wind-down pint of Hammonds Bitter.

But today, there had been a slight hitch in that well-practised routine.

On this occasion, the smooth running of the picture show had not been its usual embodiment of efficiency and organisation. This had been as a direct result of the Projectionist's negligence in loading reel number three of "The War Wagon" [starring John Wayne and Robert Mitchum] *before* reel two had been shown.

As the 16mm projector whirred into life and animated images appeared on the screen, there had been chunters and murmurs from down below in the auditorium.

Meaningful stares were directed up to the projection room and this alerted me to my mistake.

Switching off the projector and hastily rewinding, I leaned out of the projection room doors and shouted a Very Important Announcement to the audience:

"Now, ladies and gentlemen, pretend that you haven't seen that bit. Just forget all about it, and we'll start again - in the right place..."

As public performances go, this represented a pretty poor standard. But, God Bless 'Em, the children of Earlsheaton accepted my gross negligence with good grace as they accredited it to my already lengthy list of Daft Educational Mistakes.

The chuntering and muttering stopped and the film rolled towards its dramatic conclusion, thirty minutes later than scheduled. Sure enough, as the credits roll and the house-lights brighten, the kids make their ways out of the Hall and out of the school doors.

Down the tree-lined school drive, the sounds of their re-anactments gradually fade on the night air, leaving behind a silent, empty school. Empty, that is, except for the Projectionist / Usherette / Caretaker.

The Projectionist completes his professional duties and packs away the images of the Hollywood Dream Factory into their heavy black boxes, ready for despatch to the film hire company the following day.

The Usherette counts up all the 10 pee's, bags them up and locks them in an office drawer for the night. All that remains now is for the Caretaker to perform a safety check of the Hall, and all three of us can go home, via The Whistler.

Silence reigns as I descend the narrow staircase of the projection room and make my way into the Hall through the vast, wooden doors.

Some thoughtful person has already turned out all the roof lights, so the vast auditorium is now only lit through the great windows which form one wall down the left-hand side. An eerie night-time glow filters through these windows, casting long, indistinct shadows across the stage apron some thirty yards away.

Outside, there is no sound, save for the faint moan of the night breeze way above me in the rafters.

Casting round in Caretaker Mode, ready to lock up and depart, I notice that a side-door onto the stage-apron is open, so I instinctively make my way towards it. The light switches are behind me, outside on the corridor.

"I can see well enough by the light of the windows," I decide - uncharacteristically.

Bravely ignoring the fact that it *is* dark and I *am* completely and utterly alone, I decide to tough it out and to make the long walk down the centre aisle. I take a few cautious steps in the semi-darkness...

And then I see it!

The stage-curtains rustle and whisper as they part at the proscenium arch. There is a moan of rushing wind from above and a long silvery shape appears out of the wings. It glides half-way across the apron in an eerie silence and hovers centre-stage.

My eyes bulge wide in trembling fear.

All the childhood memories of Johnny Goblin and The White-Haired Old Gentleman in Red come rushing back.

The sweat of terrified dread breaks out on my terror-wracked forehead. I turn and run in a blind panic towards the double-doors at the back.

Crashing through them, I grope in panic for the corridor light-switches. Yanking them on, I come to rest, leaning against the wall, heaving and panting, trying to control my terrified, shaking limbs.

I expect the worst - a haunting, demonic attack by the phantom as it makes its ghostly way round the school. I brace myself for the moment when the great doors will burst open...

For ten minutes or so I remain braced.

The silence is deafening. From somewhere in the ether above me, the throb of my heartbeat pounds in my eardrums and my knees meet each other in a regular staccato rhythm. My mouth is dry and my teeth chatter as I await my fate.

But nothing happens.

Thoughts of Johnny Goblin begin to fade away; The Old White-Haired Gentleman in Red recedes on the ghostly air-waves back to Greenland; the pounding in my ears subsides. Stretching out a still shaking arm, I risk a peep into the Hall round the edge of one of the great doors. It opens with a groan and a creak.

In the auditorium, all is quiet and still.

The ghostly half-light from the windows falls wanly across the rows of wooden-backed chairs which are primed and ready for tomorrow's assembly. One of them lies where I left it, overturned in the centre aisle as I made my frantic dash for safety only a few minutes ago.

I force every sinew of my terrified being to look towards the stage-apron. I see the curtains wafting gently against the proscenium arch. Someone/Something has just brushed them aside to leave the stage-apron and exit, stage left. Of this I am certain!

So I turn tail and scarper.

Past the Boss's Office, down the steps and out of the Main School Doors, slamming them behind me.

A frantic fumbling with my bunch of keys, a desperately swift turn of the key in the lock and I am off, not even bothering to pause for a peep as I pass alongside the great windows of the Hall.

I sprint up the banking to the nearest school wall, scale it and clear it in one smooth, terrified leap. With knees whirring like bee's wings, I leg it down the narrow ginnel beside Crown Flatts Rugby Ground and out onto Canterbury Road.

Leg-muscles fuelled by the adrenalin rush of abject fear, I shoot up Bywell Road. In no time at all, my cold, clammy hand is fastened round a pint in The Whistler. I take a long swig of the life-restoring nectar and heave a huge sigh of relief.

With still-shaking hands, I nervously fumble to light a Woodbine.

"What's up with thee," asks Jack, one of the locals next to me at the bar. "Tha looks as if tha's seen a ghooast."

"Ah 'ave, Jack," I whisper hoarsely, lapsing into Shoddy Town Speak.

"Just now... In t' schooil 'all ...Crossin' t'stage, it wor. All shiny an' shekkin'."

Jack shakes a disbelieving head and with a mocking smile, returns to his pint of Guinness.

"Pull t'other one - it spits," he laughs.

Indignantly, I return to Teacher-Speak. "In all honesty, Jack! I've just seen it with my own eyes. The Ghost of Earlsheaton School. Walking across the stage, silvery and trembling in all its awesome glory. Honestly, I *have* seen it."

But in the warm comforting glow of The Whistler's Saloon Bar, the first doubts begin to surface...

"At least, I *think* I have..."

***

I'LL GET YOU BACK

I'm a fan of the "You're Only Here Once" principle. You know the one I mean. It's the one that says "You've only got one shot at this life, pal, so you might as well treat others as you'd want 'em to treat you." Besides, Life has an uncanny way of paying you back exactly what you deserve, so it's probably best to make sure that you've a clean slate at all times.

Perhaps you'll get my drift when I tell you this particular Shoddy Town tale. It starts in the cloakrooms at Batley Grammar School in 1962 and it ends under the stage at Earlsheaton High School about twenty years later...

On Friday mornings, in 1962, we first year sixth form members of the Batley Grammar School KOYLI CCF* who had any distance to travel by bus, would do so in "civvies". For this, there was a very simple reason.

The two years previous [when we'd been in the Fourth and Fifth Years], BGS Law stated that all cadets on active service with the CCF on Friday afternoons, had to travel to school on Friday morning in full battle-dress uniform. So undertaking your journey in head-to-toe KOYLI kit, your green beret singling you out like a Belisha Beacon on the high street, you presented an easy target to all the witty wags on board your bus. Just as with all the other lads who travelled to school from the far regions of Gomersal or Ossett, my end-of-week morning journey from Liversedge was Purgatory itself.

Each Friday am, without fail, the moment I'd stepped on

---

* King's Own Yorkshire Light Infantry Combined Cadet Force

board the Heavy Woollen District Transport Company's vehicle for the journey to the bottom of Carlinghow Hill, I'd been swamped by an incessant tide of ridicule, cat-calls and snide mickey-taking. In my case, it was all the Heckmondwike Grammar School kids on the top deck who did the business. They were brim-full of barbed sarcasm about my appearance, primed and ready for my arrival on the top deck. On some occasions, however, I met my first barrage on the rear platform - from the bus conductor. Some of them were at it, too:

A little sparkle lights up the navy-blue uniformed face at the bottom of the stairs as the big red bus squeaks to a halt outside the Bar House.

"Nar then, Montgomery," sneers the navy-blue uniform. "Are we travelling half-fare today? Cheap travel for Servicemen, is it, eh?" And all the Heckmondwike Grammar School kids, listening in from the top-deck, would fall out of their maroon, upholstered seats in helpless mirth.

Squirming in adolescent embarrassment all the way up the stairs, I walk straight into a fresh salvo of banter:

"Them's a reight pair o' pants, is them, Freddie. Aster got somebody else in theer wi' thi? Is that why tha's to wear them things rahnd thi ankles - to stop 'oo-ever it is escapin'?"

If only the below-stairs luggage compartment were big enough to swallow me up - whole and out of sight!

For seeing out 1960 and 1961 in the face of such grave adolescent danger, you deserved, at the very least, a KOYLI Cadet Military Medal for Bravery. Eventually we military-minded travellers on board the Number 20 bus

[Leeds-Mirfield via Batley] decided to put a stop to all the Clever Dick remarks and painful urine-extraction...

Upon reaching the ripe old age of seventeen and, along with it, attaining First Year Sixth Form status, we were accorded some measure of mature responsibility in our Friday morning travel arrangements. This meant that we could keep our battle-dress uniforms in our lockers/cupboards/desks at school during the week.

When the 3-20pm bell announced the start of Friday's CCF timetable, we would dash down to the cloakrooms, change into khaki drill and nip smartly onto the front yard parade ground for the muster.

Nobody seemed to mind and it saved us endless hours of Friday morning red-faced ridicule on the bus to school. Soon, vast numbers of the Friday morning CCF Travelling Contingent from the Far Regions cottoned on to the idea, and the whole process became a matter of routine.

No more jibes and insults were slung our way, the Heckmondwike Grammar School kids aboard my bus started ganging up on each other instead of insulting me, and the whole scenario changed dramatically.

Free from a weekly roasting at the hands of the passengers and conductors aboard the bus, we could concentrate on more pressing internal matters i.e. giving some other poor, unsuspecting, unfortunate sod in the CCF a right good BGS ribbing. Now, as it happened, in 1962 it was a kid called Harte.

Harte was a swot from Birstall. Bespectacled, diminutive and utterly wholesome, he was one of those A-form boys who had been accelerated academically as a result of their immense cleverness. They'd actually skipped a year's schooling, taken GCE Ordinary Level a year early and ended up, a year younger and still wet behind the ears, in the same sixth form group as us.

In general, they were an acceptable bunch of BGS lads, despite their undoubted academic prowess, but we plodders from the Alpha form, who'd entered the Sixth by the more conventional route, eyed them with some typical Shoddy Town suspicion. After all, they'd been earmarked as being "very clever" by the BGS Establishment, so they didn't enjoy our immediate, wholesome respect.

Notwithstanding all that, there were some notable characters amongst them.

The brilliant cartoonist Sam Sykes could embellish the cover of any carelessly guarded exercise book in the twinkling of an eye. Malcolm Jackson was a studious academic type who rode the slings and arrows of our unceasing ribbing with a permanently resigned smile.

But the boy Harte was a very different kettle of fish...

For one thing, he had a centre-parting in his dark, Brylcreemed hair which made his entire persona ooze "swot".

And for another, he was *always* neatly turned out in regulation blazer and smart grey flannels. He found it extremely difficult to cope with the fact that now he was a Sixth Former, he was no longer required by BGS Law to wear a school cap on his way to and from school. He kept it neatly tucked away at the bottom of his swot's satchel, ready for use when none of the Lads That Mattered were around. But his major fault was in failing to understand our "Lads That Mattered" philosophy of life. He did not realise that, in our view of things, these academically gifted young promotees were "nobbuts". They were never going to achieve our Sixth Form status as long as they'd had ink in their Conway-Stewarts*. They were always going to be socially a year behind, unable to command a place in the form hierarchy.

But one or two of them - Harte in particular - had got hold of completely the wrong end of the BGS stick...

He tried to join in with our banter and adolescently brash behaviour! He'd make unsuitably wet comments during our "men-of-the-world" conversations about the important things in life viz. Smoking, Drinking and Women.

Hanging about on the edge of our group with an obsequious grin on his moonish young face, he'd volunteer sensible observations about our manly talk:

Lad That Matters: "Oh, dusta know, Ah went aht last neet - dahn to t'Anchor - an' Ah supped ten pints afore Ah copped t'bus ooam."

Harte: "I've heard that the intake of alcohol affects your brain for up to three days afterwards. So you don't function properly at school."

Such know-all remarks were received with stoney silence and withering looks. Despite our best efforts to shun him from our "Lads That Mattered" group, he clung on doggedly and it became extremely difficult to shake him off.

We gave him a derogatory nick-name - Harte the Farte - and told him to his face - but he even refused to accept that! His dogged resilience was enviable and in the end,

---

* A superior quality fountain pen with screw top and mottled barrel, the very embodiment/badge of honour of a swot.

someone had to take summary and decisive action. And that juicy opportunity fell to Mike North [my Best Mate at school and a Life-Long Friend] and Yours Truly. It presented itself in the cloakrooms below the Dining Room one Friday afternoon, just before the CCF muster, and we took full advantage...

Like the rest of us who'd volunteered to serve Queen and Country in the CCF, Harte had taken Sixth Form privilege to which he'd no technical right. He'd developed the upstart habit of arriving on Friday mornings in civvies, just like the rest of us. And then, just like us, he'd change into his RAF Section blue uniform in time for CCF activities. Down in the cloakrooms, he'd divest himself of his BGS blazer, smartly-pressed grey flannels and his Conway-Stewart and hang them all on one of the pegs at the back.

On this particular occasion, Mike and I had decided that it was one of those Friday afternoons which merited leaving school at 3.20pm. We'd worked extremely hard all week, hadn't we? We'd proudly handed in our English essays on time to Irving L. Theaker, hadn't we? We were mature Sixth formers, weren't we? This was the fag-end of the academic week, wasn't it? So now was the time to scarper - and stuff those CCF activities.

We'd trod this same path many times before.

Collect all week-end requirements, wait in the cloakrooms for Friday's last period to get under way. Walk brazenly out of the front door of the school, hard by our Herbert Coulter Form Room and proceed across the Mud Bath. Arrive at Mike's house in Stanley Terrace where we would relax in style, coffee and Woodbines a-plenty, lolling back in the arm-chairs, listening to his records.

This time, it was no different. We sneaked surreptitiously into the cloakrooms and parked our nethers on one of the benches beneath the rows of hooks at the back. It was time to keep quiet and out of sight until lessons and CCF activities got under way.

But who is this, making his cheery way into the cloakroom?

Yes, it's obsequious, fawning Harte the Farte, all prepared to change into his Brylcreem Boy blue uniform. Mike and I look at each other in exasperation whilst we anticipate our getaway. There is nothing for it but to sit it out until the coast is completely clear.

H. the F. burbles on enthusiastically about flying gliders, the techniques of which he was going to be learning today and towards which he was looking very forward. Throughout the process of doing up his tunic buttons, tying his tie and doing up his flies, he twitters on in top gear, till Mike and I would have gladly throttled him there and then. But we put up with all the meaningless twittering because we didn't want to give priggish, perfect Harte the slightest hint about what we were up to.

At last, after carefully measuring the angle of his RAF beret with a protractor, he made a corrective adjustment to his headgear, straightened his tie by careful reference to a slide-rule - and departed for the muster.

To this day, I do not know whose idea it was. It came in the twinkling of a mischievous eye as Mike and I both spotted Harte's civvie trousers hanging limply on a cloakroom rail.

We nodded to each other knowingly and removed the trousers from their snug little peg. Finding a scruffy, dirty, un-used locker in the dark recesses of a caretaker's store-cupboard, we rammed those trousers deep into a corner, far out of sight - and scarpered.

Out of the school front-door by the Herbert Coulter Room, crossing Carlinghow Hill, we chortled with glee. All the way over the Mud Bath and right on to Stanley Terrace, we giggled fitfully, picturing the hapless Farte desperately searching for his leg-gear at 5pm that evening.

The bravado of our daring escapade even kept us chuckling throughout the following week-end.

At Dorothy's Coffee Bar on the end of Commercial Street, the report of our cloakroom activities livened up the Friday night atmosphere of tobacco, espresso and juke-box rock n' roll. In the Saturday morning changing rooms, it brought raucous guffaws from the First XI stalwarts. It even revived the doom and gloom of Sunday evening and the sad prospect of the coming week's return to school...

Monday morning arrived and the members of Lower Sixth [Modern] gathered for early morning registration with form master K.C. [Ken] Fitchett.

Eagerly anticipating a nine o'clock English lesson with Irving L. Theaker and the literary delights contained within chapter three of Jane Austen's "Emma", Mike and I were somewhat taken aback when Fitchett clears his throat and demands everyone's full attention. An expectant silence fell on the gathering.

"A somewhat unsavoury incident occurred on Friday evening, " announces Ken, eyes half-shut and addressing the ceiling of the Herbert Coulter Room. "It has come to my notice that a member of the form had to travel home to Birstall in the greatest distress - without his trousers..."

Simultaneously, Mike and I create the same mental picture:

Harte mounts the platform of the big red Heavy Woollen District Transport Company Omnibus on a busy Friday tea-time. His satchel is stuffed full of all his swot's material for weekend homework. His Conway-Stewart is firmly clipped in the top pocket of his BGS blue blazer. But below the belt, he is clad only in his underpants.

We savour the prospect of an entire passenger complement of the busy tea-time bus laughing in derisory fashion at the sight of Harte in his underpants. We guffaw inwardly but maintain poker faces.

"That person," continues Fitchett, dramatically, "was Harte, and he believes his trousers were stolen by someone in this room. I feel that whoever it may have been ought to have the decency and sense of fair play to own up."

The silence is thick now as we wait expectantly but, at this point, a wave of selfish cowardice engulfs me. If I were to confess to the heinous crime, I stood to lose a great deal.

I'd only just managed to hold on to a school place some time back in the Fourth year when I'd been shopped for throwing lighted boot-laces one Saturday night in the Palace cinema in Heckmondwike. My Dad had had to plead with F.W. Scott [Headmaster] for my grammar school status and I'd escaped expulsion by the skin of my teeth.

Over the intervening years, I'd managed to live down the shame of that incident, build up my good character credentials and become accepted by pupils and staff alike as a steady sort of chap. Now, I was in line for a Prefect's badge, and that bubble would burst asunder if I were to come clean about the Farte's leggings.

In the silence that followed Fitchett's request, we all kept shtumm.

"Harte himself has a fair idea of the culprit," continued Fitchett, "but I feel it would be far better for all concerned if the perpetrator were to come forward. I leave you to your thoughts on the matter." And he swept out of the room.

Mike and I met outside on the black-and-white tiled corridor.

"What's a perpetrator?" I ask, puzzled.

"Buggered if I know," says Mike. "But did yer see Harte the Farte lookin' at us. The swine's offter drop us in it, Ah can tell... But not if we get there first."

"Ow d'yer mean," I wail, still puzzled.

"We 'aveter own up afore 'e gets 'is three penn'orth in."

"Burr Ah dadn't. Ah've ter much ter lose. Ah weeant be a Prefect - an' Ah might gerr expelled," I whine pathetically.

And at this point in his school career, Mike becomes a BGS Hero [First Class].

In an act of unselfish dedication to the Truth and to standing up for what he believed to be Right and Proper, he takes the entire blame for the incident himself.

He owns up to Fitchett, receives admonishment from F.W Scott, and is scrubbed from the list of runners and riders in the Prefects' Badge Stakes. And what is more, *he never utters one syllable of my name in connection with the prank.*

In the fullness of time, I receive my prefect's badge and my reputation remains unsullied.

I spend the rest of my life, however, admiring Mike's courage and heroism in facing up to the consequences which I dodged in cowardly fashion. More importantly, I admire his friendship and trust.

But the Great Controller of Life made a careful note in his Outstanding Debts Ledger that summer in 1962:

"*I'll get you back,*" he recorded, in red ink. "*The time will come...*"

And He filed the reference until a later date...

***

It's 1970 now, and I'm well into my teaching career at Earlsheaton School. I've made another life-long pal in David Moss who is Head of Physical Education. Along with him and that other cheeky chappy, David Croft, it is my privilege to cavort around many a Shoddy Town football field on Saturday afternoons as we represent the interests of Wheelwright Old Boys AFC in the Yorkshire Old Boys League.

Now, as it happens, Mossie is also a very talented writer and entertainer. In a rush of blood to the cerebral area one Summer Term, he suggests that we write a school pantomime for production the following Christmas.

Such an act of bravado involved us in summer holiday hours of endless amusement writing a suitably school-orientated script. This was closely followed by hours of after-school rehearsing with staff and pupils during the

Autumn Term. The Christmas productions were fairly amateurish, but as they progressed, year on year, they were enormous fun.

By 1976, the annual school pantomime had become a fixture in the school calendar, and Yours Truly was in charge.

Now, as luck would have it, Earlsheaton School is equipped with one of the best stage set-ups in the locality.

Built as a community centre in the early 1950's, the vast auditorium that is the school hall looks onto a huge proscenium arch stage equipped with all the theatrical machinery you could wish for as a budding producer.

There was space above the stage for "flying" sets, a lighting gallery stuffed full of technical equipment, and there was a trap-door in the stage floor leading to a scenery store below. Leading off from this was a network of service tunnels which weaved, web-like, underneath the whole school.

Needless to say, we amateurs took full advantage of such professional facilities, unlikely to ever meet their likes again in our teaching careers.

Sets and back-cloths were laboriously constructed so that we could "fly" them, thus regaling our Earlsheaton school audiences *ad nauseam* with umpteen set changes per production. And, in December 1976, the set of "Babes in the Wood" is primed and ready for its release on the general public.

But, like most things in life, there was a hidden extra to all this. You see, that stage held a closely guarded secret amongst the pupils of Earlsheaton school.

Unknown to any members of staff, some very naughty Fourth Year boys had discovered the afore-mentioned labarynth of service tunnels running below the school. And they had also discovered that you could access these tunnels by lifting off the stage trap-door, dropping the ten feet or so into the scenery store and setting off on your merry way.

It was pitch-black, damp and very dirty work, crawling about in all the filth, but it was better than incarceration in a classroom any day of the school week...

Now, on this particular occasion, the said bunch of lads had decided that an hour's worth of Mathematics at the end of the school day was not a prospect charged with a vast amount of exciting fun. They'd indulged in that age-old pastime of suspending educational activities for a brief period. Just like Mike and I on Friday afternoons when we were in the Sixth Form.

But *they* hadn't left the premises and gone home - like so many of their compatriots. No, *this* gang had decided to do some exploring.

Roaming the school in secret, they'd crept unnoticed down the corridor beside the Hall and up onto the stage. Standing in the middle of the dimly lit set, Macker, a stocky, round lad with black curly hair, whispers dramatically: "What we bahna do nar?"

Indicating the trap-door, wiry, weasel-faced Piggy outlines the current mission:

"Ah've 'eared as tha can get darn yon 'oil and walk abaht under t'schooil, in all t'tunnels," he hissed. "So that's what we're ofter do. Come on, lerrus ger agate."

They lift the metal trap-door rings, slide the cover back

and down they go. Dropping deftly into the darkness they land on the floor of the scenery store.

A quick check of their bearings tells them which service tunnel will take them away under the main corridor. Off they creep on all fours, ducking a vast array of pipes and wires, and they wend their naughty way into the deep, dank blackness.

During the next hour or so, until the end of the school day, they crawled about in the pitch darkness, chortling with adolescent glee at their brazen bravado and cheek. Every so often, they cock an expectant ear to ascertain which classroom they might be under. Jenner even makes a few ghost noises to add to the fun.

The jape comes to an abrupt end, however, when, after a crawl of a hundred or so arduous yards, Macker just makes out the klaxon clang of the four o'clock bell on the corridor above. He makes an executive decision there and then that it's home time.

Adjudging their position with uncanny accuracy to be immediately under the exit trap at the Canterbury Road entrance doors, Macker shouts to the others:

"Come on, lads! It's time we buggered off." And he heaves at the steel trap-door above his head.

Up above, in the Canterbury Road entrance hall, school is out. The last ringing notes of the best school bell of the day are just fading away and a tidal wave of youthful humanity is hitting the corridors.

Kids are milling everywhere and there is an air of fresh expectancy which accompanies the heart-felt release from a pent-up classroom. Some of the older lads are hanging about near the great staircase waiting for their mates; the older girls are hanging about outside the Geography Room waiting for the older lads who are waiting for their mates; the littler kids are chasing out of the school door. They are not hanging about for anybody. There is a cacophany of noisy glee.

"G'night, miss," chirp one or two of the younger ones as they pass Miss Middlemarch, a young teacher of Religious Education, who is on duty just inside the Canterbury Road entrance.

Slightly built but very neat and trim in appearance, Miss M. is following to the letter, the Standing Orders from her Staff Handbook entitled "Procedure at the End of the School Day". She has taken up station at the appointed place "next to the Canterbury Road entrance doors, to supervise the safe exit of pupils onto Canterbury Road".

For the next ten minutes, she stands on the same spot, bang in the middle of *that* trap-door which is set into the red tiles of the corridor floor.

Down below, Macker is heaving upwards with all his Fourth Year might.

"Oh, gie us an 'and, Piggy," he calls. "Else wes'll be darn 'ere all neet."

Together, the pair of them heave and strain until the trap-door finally begins to lift...

Whilst on duty above, Miss Middlemarch has been mulling over a recent lesson about the Ascension with some Third Year kids. She feels a sudden surge of emotion as, completely unassisted, she herself rises some eight or nine inches from the floor. She is carried off in a transport of delight as her own personal ascension continues for another foot or so before the trap-door beneath her feet tips over and she lands in a disappointed heap on the corridor floor.

She is at ground level as Macker's soot-blackened, cob-webbed face beams out at her from the depths of the service tunnel.

"Sorry, miss," he grins. "We thowt it wor time for us ter be gerrin off ooam..."

***

"But where," I hear you ask, "does the Great Controller of Life fit into all this?"

The answer to that question lies behind those velvetybrown stage curtains the very next day which is heralded by a sunny December morning.

During dress rehearsal of our pantomime the day before, a minor problem to do with the position of a stage flat had arisen. In order to attend to the matter, I'd taken it upon myself that morning to duck the daily treat that was the Headmaster's assembly.

If I was quiet about it, I'd be able to sort out the problem while the Boss is giving his morning address, return to my station at the back of the Hall in time for the end of the assembly - and no-one would be any the wiser...

I'd made my quiet way down the corridor beside the Hall, up the back-stage steps and onto the set.

By now, the muster is in full swing. Files of children make their way into the Hall accompanied by their Form Tutors. With due decorum some three hundred and fifty adolescent bums have been manoeuvred into position on the old, unforgiving, steel-framed chairs. A reverential silence begins to permeate the auditorium as I picture the scene from the stage wings.

The Hall is full of sleep-logged children and staff, all eagerly anticipating the Headmaster's latest assembly offering. He strides up the impressive steps, onto the stage-apron in front of the curtain and begins a moral tale.

A complete silence falls on the assembled gathering.

Behind the curtain, the stage is in darkness, save for one emergency light deep in the wings behind me. In order to inspect the position of the offending stage flat, I would have to tip-toe across the stage only feet away from the pontificating Headmaster. But, of course, I would be completely out of sight, hidden by the curtain.

In the sombre darkness of the set, I could just about make out the other side of the stage where I wanted to be. Carefully and cautiously, I set off.

Taking slow and measured steps, painstakingly placing one foot in front of the other, I crept in utter silence towards the gloom on the other side of the stage. Nobody in the auditorium must hear a sound; the entire exercise must be completed with a total noise-blackout, or I'd be responsible for fouling up the Boss's carefully planned assembly...

Feeling daringly smug about my progress so far, I half-considered a wager with myself to see how close I could get to the Boss on the other side of the curtain as he continued his assembly.

Perhaps I could do a Morecambe and Wise entrance from

behind the drapes to liven things up a bit? I decided to forego that pleasure and continued my slow, painstaking journey across the centre of the stage.

The sensation of taking a meticulously executed, slow and controlled step in darkness, and placing a careful foot on fresh air is almost indescribable.

For a fleeting second, I thought I was drunk as my body shot forward and downward at the same time.

Maintaining self-discipline until the last, I descended the ten feet into the scenery store in utter silence, to land on some old gym-mats which had been dumped out of the way for the duration.

On the way down, my hip caught the edge of the wooden edging round the open trap-door ripping the belt clean off my trousers. The only sound, however, was the tearing of my shirt as it caught on a loose splinter.

In a heap on the gym-mats, I was utterly flabbergasted as to the events of the preceeding ten seconds or so. What on earth had happened?

For a minute or two, I lay prone and tried to work out where I was and who was with me. In the thick darkness above, I could just detect the muffled sounds of the Boss's continuing assembly, so at least nobody had been disturbed by my fall from grace.

But how had I got here? Which crazy pillock had left the trap-door off? How in Hell's name was I going to get out?

The Great Controller of Life chuckled mischievously and ticked off the entry in His Book:

... a meticulously executed, slow and controlled step in darkness ...

INVOICE

To: F.A. BUTLER

Repayment of Dirty trick played by F.Butler on Harte the Farte,
November 1962

Payment due from truanting boys at Earlsheaton School,
December 1976

He got me back alright.

Perhaps if I'd come clean about my trick in 1962, those
1976 lads might have replaced the trap-door. I wouldn't
have been stuck down a dark, dank hole nursing my
wounds, and my trip across the dark stage would have
remained uneventful.

But now, it was all stacking up.

For pinching Harte the Farte's grey school flannels and for
failing to own up, I am condemned to die, deep down in
this stinking, dark, damp scenery store. There are rats and
all kinds of vermin down here to devour my rotting bones.
And I must depart this world in silence, for fear of
interrupting the Boss's assembly.

From ten feet above, a thin, weak ray of light filters down
to me and I can just make out the shape of the trap-door
opening. The pain in my side is beginning to throb and I
fancy there's a trickle of blood running down my forehead.
I cast around in the dark and find an old stage box which
I drag beneath the opening.

Staggering about in the darkness, but managing to tip-toe
in silence the while, I manage to drag my pain-wracked
frame onto the box. With a super-human effort, I grip the
ledge above me and haul my carcass up through the trap-
door onto the floor of the stage above.

Breathless and in mortal anguish, I strain my ears for any sound of rescue. Fifteen feet away, on the other side of those stage-curtains, the Headmaster has just exhorted the assembled gathering to prayer. A hallowed silence has settled throughout the School Hall.

If I shout for help now, a wail from the depths of the stage will undoubtedly make them all think that, at last, the Holy Spirit has descended on Earlsheaton. The Hall will clear in a frenzied dash for refuge and I will be bound for a spell of Eternal Damnation. So I slowly and painfully [but maintaining complete radio silence] drag my injured carcass across the stage and into the wings.

I grope for the side-exit door and stagger down the steps onto the side corridor.

My face is soot-blackened, my forehead bleeding and, beneath my dust-covered jacket, my shirt is ripped asunder. My trousers are torn at the knee and my tie has worked its way round my neck to hang limply over my shoulder. Quite clearly, to any observer, I have been the victim of a brutal and savage attack.

The rising tide of noise in the auditorium tells me that Assembly is over for another day and that the headmaster will be making his way out of the Hall through the great wooden doors at the back. I should just about catch him before he crosses the corridor into his office to tell him about the dastardly deeds of yesterday's truanters. He will, of course, be overcome with professional compassion and sympathy as he witnesses, at first hand, my bruised and battered state. Something will have to be done about this unfortunate chain of events. The culprits will have to be found and punished ...

Slowly and agonisingly, I limp round the corner of the corridor just as the great Hall door swings open and the begowned Headmaster sweeps out.

He halts, turns and casts an imperious, inspectorial glance over my dishevelled and battered frame.

"Good morning, Mr Butler," he mutters and, without so much as a "What the hell happened to you," he sweeps past me across the corridor and disappears into his office.

***

The Great Controller of Life makes the final entry in His Book:

Payment received in full
With thanks

***

JUDGEMENT DAY

The sunlight blasted through the curtains and woke me from a fitful, nerve-wracked sleep. The first day of my *proper* working life had dawned at last.

I leapt out of bed and donned my teacher's uniform - black barathea blazer with its University of London badge emblazoned on the pocket; grey flannels neatly pressed; and a *nice* pair of brown suede shoes. Fearful of being late for my baptismal day at the chalk-face, I shot downstairs for my scrambled-eggs.

After a cheery wave to my Mum, I made my way down to the Bar House, as I had done for the duration of my school career. And just as in days of yore, I waited to catch the Number 20 bus [Mifield-Leeds via Batley] to the bottom of Field Hill.

But today was different.

Alighting into the morning sunshine on Bradford Road, close by Mad Jack's and his threepenny Woodbines of yester-year, I begin a brisk walk up the steep hill. I have joined a host of boys, some small, some fat and some as big as me, as we surge in a tidal wave of humanity up the steep slope. Looking about me, I am a little disconcerted.

My red-faced embarrassment stems from the fact that we are dressed almost identically.

We're all smartly turned out in black blazers and grey flannels - I even spot the odd pair of nice brown suede shoes. For a few moments, I blend inconspicuously with a crowd of schoolboys returning from their annual summer break. I have to own up to feeling a bit of a pillock.

I'm supposed to be a teacher now, I reason loftily with myself. I should be set apart from the pupils - the hoi polloi whom I am about to face from the other side of the old school desk. Yet here I am, unidentifiable in a raucous crowd of uniformed youngsters. Tomorrow, I vow to myself, I shall wear my green checked sports jacket and brown trousers...and buy a car.

The tidal wave surges onwards and upwards with me in its depths. We negotiate the even steeper rise of Blenheim Drive at the top of which our paths diverge. As the tidal wave makes its way round to the back of the school, I sail off in a north-westerly direction towards the hallowed portals of Batley Boys' High School Main Entrance.

Gasping for breath after such an early-morning bout of exercise, I prepared for my encounter with George Christopher Locke [Headmaster], Form 3 and a brand-new teaching career...

Only minutes later, I was in front of a class of eleven year old Shoddy Town lads, all gazing expectantly at their new teacher. I cleared a very nervous throat and began my postive and enthusiastic speech of welcome to my new charges.

Prattling on about behaviour and timetables and homework, I was just beginning to get into my educational stride and to feel reasonably pleased with my performance so far, when a fair-haired, round-faced lad grunted a blunt enquiry from somewhere in the middle of the classroom:

"Sir, worrabout mi dinner money?"

A vital educational question, requiring an immediate answer. I stifled my immediate response: "Oh, shit! I've forgotten to collect it," and cleared a nervous throat. I was about to make my very first schoolmasterly pronouncement:

"If I were you, Holroyd, I'd put it away until Sir starts collecting it."

For the time being, Holroyd seemed satisfied with my solution to his problem, so I proceeded with my awkward, amateurish introductory talk to the class.

Now, as I glance back over my nostalgic, educational shoulder, I realise that my pronouncement regarding Holroyd's financial predicament was probably the very first of many situations throughout my career when I was called upon to make some kind of judgement. Little did I realise it then, but for the next thirty years, a prominent feature of my working life would be the passing of such judgements in all sorts of varied educational settings. I turned out to be a sort of referee to whom folk turned in all sorts of varied situations for immediate, whistle-blowing decisions.

Children and adults would present their ultimatums to me on a daily basis, expecting instant, on-the-spot dispensation of justice, thus settling all sorts of "important" issues. After all, *I* was the teacher, wasn't I? *My* word was law enough to settle a matter, wasn't it? What *I* said, went, didn't it?

Now, I have to admit that, in all that time, I never quite caught on to the idea of exercising due caution in settling such issues. I would often dive straight in with an instant decision, not seeing the educational wood for the sociological trees. By so doing, I managed to produce many minor and some major catastrophes, often on a daily basis...

In the hurly-burly of classroom life, both at Batley High School *and* at Earlsheaton, quite the naughtiest children I ever came across were known in both schools by the names: "Worrim" and his sister "Worrer".

"Who threw that on the floor?"

"Sir, it *Worrim.*"

or

"Who made that awful noise?"

"Sir, it *Worrer.*"

On these occasions, judgement was swift and summary. In the early days at Batley: "Right, it Worrim, worrit? Bend over, lad and have a dose of Watt Fore*."

Later, at Earlsheaton: "Right, it Worrer, worrit? Detention for you, my girl."

As time went by, whenever I was consulted as judge and jury in cases of dispute between children, their Mums and Dads, Aunties and Uncles, Grannies and Grandads and a host of other sociological agencies, [including next-door's dog], I learned to temper my approach. I didn't dive in quite so abruptly and always dodged and weaved in order to give myself some valuable thinking time.

As I prepare to face up to today's angry parent, memories of a bleached bedroom carpet creep to the surface and the successful invented-excuses technique is at the fore-

---

* My pet name for a size 12 gym shoe. "If you misbehave in my class, you get what for." As a long-term disciplinary measure, it's use was utterly unsuccesful.

front of my thinking. This belt-and- braces, sleeves-rolled-up, stubble-chinned bricklayer sticks out his defiant chin across my office desk.

"Nar, look 'ere, Mr Butler. Tha'r t'bloody taycher, aren't yer? Nar, yon Jezzer's bin smackin' my little Bernard on't way ooam fro' t'schooil, so tha's ter deal wi' it. Ah can't be wi' ar Bernard all t'time e's out o' t' house, so wot *tha* bahna do abaht it, mester, eh?"

Sensing myself being cornered into meting out rough justice, I buy some time:

"Well now, Mr Longbottom. I fully appreciate what you're saying. [*prepares to "flannel" for a while and enters Risk Assessment Phase*]

"But after all, this *is* happening on the way home from school and *we* haven't instructed "yon Jezzer" to smack your Bernard, have we? We don't run classes in bullying at this school. So quite what you'd like me to do about it isn't clear. Perhaps we might hang this Jezzer from the school gate after a session of suitable torture by the PE staff? Or perhaps the Science department could rig up an electric chair for him?"

There were many encounters of such a nature, when the complainants demanded instant justice which, in truth, I was unable to deliver.

Often, as on this occasion, they would leave with the threat of vigilante activity:

"Ah'm off rahnd theer terneet an' Ahs'll gie t'little bugger a thick ear mesen."

So the idea of hedging one's bets in the judgement-passing stakes was one which should have become second nature after a few years at the chalk face. But what about when it happens to *you*, and you're not in the safe haven of your classroom or office? What happens if you're out in the Big Wide World and Judgement Day arrives, calling for you to make a snap decision, based on what you see?

Well, it's not easy, I can tell you, and it happened to me early on in my career, and it taught me a lesson for life...

Now, even though I say it myself, I used to fancy myself as a bit of an amateur actor. Nothing serious, you understand - a few walk-on parts with the Heckmondwike Players and several comic roles with the Dewsbury Arts Group - usually as a member of the Armed Forces alongside my good friend and *very* accomplished thespian, Terry Ryan. That was about my theatrical lot.

It was extremely good fun, and the plaudits after a performance were usually enough to satisfy my pathetic theatrical ego.

On the occasion of the afore-mentioned Judgement Day, I had been rehearsing with the Dewsbury Arts Group at their Peel Street premises for a part in "Reluctant Heroes" - yet another play with a distinctly military theme.

The Arts Group had just taken over the premises - a former Quaker Meeting House - up a dark, steep, cobbled street off Bradford Road. During our preparations for performances, it was my nightly young teacher's joy to get in to an old, second-hand Vauxhall Viva via the driver's side door in the normal way. A short drive along Bradford Road brought me to Peel Street where I would park under the canopy of the day-time car-park for Saville Heaton's clothing factory.

A spot of physical agility was then required in order to

exit the vehicle because the driver's side door-handle was inoperable from inside the car.

On this occasion, I climbed gingerly across the gear-stick, as usual, and left the car via the passenger's side door. Vowing to myself that I would operate on the faulty door that week-end, I walked up to those great wooden doors.

On dark nights such as this particular one, despite the sombre gloom cast by the shadow of the once-austere building, I would step into an oasis of fun and laughter. It was a welcome escape from the faulty driver's-side door and the drudgery of marking all those lousy exercise-books - for an hour or two at least.

Along with such icons of local amateur theatre as Andrew [Archie] Madden, Barbara Ryan, David and Judith Wood, Ian Burroughs and Peter Ragan, I was privileged to cavort around, act the fool and laugh interminably under the careful, dramatic scrutiny of Russell Whiteley, the gifted producer of our current offering.

On this particular night, we'd rehearsed gleefully and laughed uproariously as Barbara Ryan set the tone for the night's activity with a chance remark.

This vivacious, auburn-haired beauty had an electrifying stage presence. She'd frightened the living daylights out of me when I'd partnered her in a ballroom scene in "Oh What a Lovely War", dancing only inches away from her half-exposed, ball-gowned bosom.

My carefully rehearsed speeches faded away into a nervous burble at the prospect of being close up tight to such a Woman of the World. And me, still damp behind the hearing-apparatus.

Tonight, the auburn bomb-shell was in humorous mood as

she reported on the health of a local celebrity of some note.

It appeared that this poor unfortunate fellow had recently been diagnosed as having contracted phlebitis..."In his sparrer," was Barbara's chance remark, at which announcement, rehearsals ground to a hilarious halt.

All males in the cast immediately bent themselves double with legs crossed. A contorted grimace wracked each face as tears filled every eye in a surge of commiserative fellow-feeling. A charged silence followed, during which we each privately fell to considering the chap's unfortunate plight.

After a few moments of respectful, silent contemplation, broken only by a hushed enquiry as to the exact nature of the disease*, irreverent and comic remarks began to permeate the gathering:

"Hey! I bet they charge him double on t'bus!"

"He might have had to have his trousers altered - an extra pocket for the offending article..."

"Do you think he has to wheel it about in a barrow?"

From thereon, at opportune moments throughout the rehearsal, any innuendo in the script which might have been construed as a reference to the male member brought activities to a howling halt. We giggled and chortled at our own individual mental pictures of a phlebitic "sparrer".

Helpless with laughter himself, our revered leader and

---

* Phlebitis in the sparrer - painful swelling in the veins of the male organ.

producer Russell wipes the tears of mirth from his cheeks and suspends rehearsal for the evening.

Still chortling, we members of the cast begin to make our way down the narrow stairs to the dark reality outside on Peel Street. Talk was still dominated by the medical theme as we bade each other farewell and went our separate ways.

In the gloom of the steep side-street, my footsteps echoed on the cobbles as I approached the concrete canopy of the S.R.Gent's car park. Ducking into the dark recesses, I make my way towards my old two-door Vauxhall Viva, fumbling for my car keys.

I make yet another mental note to operate on the faulty driver's-side door this week-end. Getting in to the vehicle presented no problem. But getting out required a session of physical wriggling and knacker-threatening injury in the crawl across the gear-stick to alight via the passenger's door. This would have to be rectified before serious injury occurred.

Pondering a session of DIY car-mechanic activity, I make my way round the back of the car and glance through the rear window. At that moment, I have a sort of a *déja vue* experience: *There was somebody sitting in the driver's seat!*

"Oh dear," says I to myself. "I must be at the wrong car. Mine must be elsewhere..." I turned to look.

Performing a very creditable Oliver Hardy double-take, I spin on my heels. A swift check of the number-plate reveals that this *is* my car and there *is* some bugger in it!

I dash round to the driver's side door and look in. There,

gazing up at me with an array of coloured wires on his lap, is a pale-faced, sandy-haired chap. His prying hands are under the steering column, a bared copper wire in each weedy hand. I boldly appraise him of the current situation:

"Oi! You!" I bawl, teacher-fashion. "This is my car!"

Sensing immediately that the game is up, the thief begins to desperately tug and yank at the driver's door-handle, but to no avail. A grim smile of smug satisfaction lights my features as I insert my key into the lock, swing open the door and, chauffeur-like, invite the thieving swine to leave the vehicle.

As he squirms his pathetic way out onto the car-park, I brace myself for a vengeful attack. I raise my arm, bunch my fist and vow to slot the robbing sod upon final exit.

He draws ever nearer. I grab him by the scruff of the neck and yank him out. To my surprise, I achieve this with little effort, because Car Thief turns out to be a puny lightweight who offers little resistance.

I pin him up against the dark recesses of the car-park's back wall and our recriminatory conversation begins:

"That's my bloody car," I hiss dramatically and am subsequently lost for words.

My lower jaw flaps open, but no threatening noises issue forth, so I fix him with my teacher's glare.

"Go easy, on me mate," whines Car Thief. "Ah've a wife and six kids. Ah've no job an' I owe a lot o' brass. Ah've tried to get work, burrit's ner good. Nob'dy'll 'ave me. Ah've just come back fro' Sheffield seekin' work, an' Ah've ner bus-fare to gerr ooam wi'..."

And his excuses proceed in like vein. I listen, with teacher-like courtesy, having released my grip on his collar.

By now, I could hear voices out on the cobbled street. Producer Russell Whiteley along with Peter Hatton, a young, shy and retiring member of the cast, [recruited for a taste of theatrical action as a bit-part Medical Orderly in "Reluctant Heroes"] had joined me under the car-park canopy.

"This bloke's been trying to pinch my car," shouts I. A a look of terror blanches the ever-decisive Russell's features and he takes off like a terrified rabbit. He races off down Peel Street onto Bradford Road and out of sight.

"What's up wi' im," asks Car Thief, obviously feeling more confident now that he is not dealing with a gang of bruisers who are about to beat the living daylights out of him.

"Don't know," replies Peter. "I think he has to get home for his supper..." and he sprawls nonchalantly across the bonnet of my car.

A thick silence followed, during which I noted Car Thief's shifty sideways glances as he assessed his best escape route.

If he were to make a break for it, he would probably get away with ease, since it was quite obvious that neither myself nor the youthful Peter Hatton had the physical attributes of Saturday night, town-centre "heavies". I braced myself for physical restraint, and scrutinized closely every movement of Car Thief's beady little eyes.

During the silence, I hear a little voice from somewhere

above my head. "But where is this scenario leading?" asks my Inner Self. " What do we do now? Do we shake hands, call it a draw and everybody goes home for tea?"

I was spared the mental anguish of solving such problems when I heard Russell's heavy breathing behind me.

"It's OK. I've called the police and they're on the way," he panted. "So we'll just have to watch him till they get here..." and he promptly collapsed exhausted across the boot of my now-disabled car.

Upon hearing Russell's news, Car Thief began pleading with us as if his very life depended on it.

"Go easy on me, fellers. Ah've ner job an' Ah didn't mean no 'arm. Ah've just got back fro' Doncaster seekin' work. Ah've a wife an' three kids at ooam waitin' fer me. Gie us a chance, mate. Ah'm just an ordinary bloke what's darn on 'is luck..."

But unfortunately for this particular felon, the die was well and truly cast.

We three stood resolutely steadfast, barring his escape. Realising that his recollection of his own whereabouts for the day had been geographically questionable, and that the size of his family was diminishing by the minute, Car Thief fell to contemplating his lot.

We had him cornered against the back wall of the car park. Behind us were two or three parked cars barring his way out. To escape, he would have to shove past all of us, thread his way through the line of vehicles and leg it down Peel Street onto Bradford Road. There was no way out...

We eyed each other warily, half expecting Car Thief to

make a run for it. Once again another thick silence descended.

Having got his breath back after the chase to the telephone, it was Russell who eventually broke the tense silence. Lapsing into producer-mode, he begins to ruminate over the evening's rehearsal.

"You know, that bit at the end of Act One where Gregory drops his trousers and the girls are under the beds..."

I turn to listen, nodding enthusiastically.

"Well, I'm convinced that it ought to have more dramatic underlining. I think we shall have to adjust the lighting to get the full effect..."

"Yes, I know what you mean Russell," I replied. Turning to the young Peter Hatton, still sitting crossed-legged on the bonnet of my car, I pontificate with authority.

"It's quite a startling dramatic moment when you enter at that point, Peter, so it needs theatrically emphasising. Don't you think so?"

Peter murmurs in agreement and throws the conversational ball back to Russell. "What does the producer do in these circumstances, Russell?"

At this point, Our Revered Leader launches into an expert technical diagnosis. "Well, I think a subtle fade-in on spotlight number three might enhance the dramatic tone of the moment."

He emphasises his point with a rounded motion of his hands.

"And I do feel the need for a slight verification of the girls' presence under the beds. Perhaps an equally subtle fade-out on a travelling spotlight would do rather nicely..."

He drifts away into a theatrical rêverie to attempt a solution to his production problem.

Car Thief is gob-struck.

He has been apprehended by three raving luvvies all wrapped up in their own sense of self-importance. They are all currently engrossed in their own little world, discussing the finer points of dramatic production. All he has to do is sneak away, quietly, surreptitiously and unnoticed, while we are absorbed in our own pretend little Land of Make-Believe. For sure, none of us would notice his disappearance until it was far too late, and he would be long gone.

But if that was the plan at the back of his Car Thief mind, the balloon soon burst into tiny little fragments. The distant sound of a police siren sounded from somewhere along Bradford Road, growing louder by the second.

A desperate look came into his beady little eyes and he began to grovel: "Aw, c'mon pal...Gie us a chance. Let me off, will yer? Worrabout me kids?"

I am wrested violently from my little Land of Make-Believe and I descend with a thump. I hear Car Thief's desperate pleas and suddenly, the entire scenario becomes crystal-clear.

I'd been thrust into a set of circumstances which I did not want and which were not of my making. I was being forced into passing a judgement about one of my fellow human-beings. I had to become a whistle-blowing referee and reach an instant decision. Only this time, I wasn't at school.

I began a rapid teacher-like appraisal of this particular poor sod's situation.

The poor, bedraggled wizened little chap, puny and sickly white, was down on his very nethers, wasn't he? Fate had dealt him a bum hand from the bottom of the pack, and he'd a set of pretty poor cards with which to play the Game of Life. His wife and kids were at home, starving and destitute, weren't they?

And here was I, ready to shop him to the police and pile further retribution upon his pathetic, weakling shoulders. Surely, he was one of Life's Unfortunates, deserving at least one more fair crack of the proverbial whip, wasn't he?

I was just about to apologise profusely for all the trouble I'd caused him and to step aside to clear the way for his escape, when the klaxon blast of the siren shattered the depths of the car park.

Flashes of blue light cast leaping shadows onto the far wall as the dark blue Ford Cortina screeched to a halt beside us.

Out jumped two hefty Boys in Blue, one sporting the silvery-grey stripes of a Sergeant. His assistant was a huge, broad-shouldered custodian with short-cropped, red hair and a jutting square jaw.

Spotting the youthful Peter Hatton with his longish hair, sitting nonchalantly on the bonnet of the car, their Bluebottle eyes lit up and they quickly put two and two together to make six.

With his junior PC hard by his shoulder, Sergeant Bluebottle strides purposefully over to our young thespian companion.

He thrusts out his Desperate Dan, black-stubbled chin and a deep-throated, menacing growl rumbles somewhere deep in his chest cavity. This rumble is finally released in a barking crescendo:

"Bloody car thief, eh?" he roars. "They're all t'same, these young uns. Yer'd think they'd know better, wouldn't yer, eh?" - and he plucks the protesting Peter bodily from his perch on my bonnet.

As the mild-mannered Peter begins to wave his arms frantically in the struggle for his very life, Junior Bluebottle reaches enthusiastically for his truncheon. With a gleeful glint in his steely eye, he senses the prospect of being able to beat the living daylights out of some would-be criminal.

In desperation, I lapse into Shoddy Town Speak, quite unbecoming for a budding young thespian from the educational ranks:

"No, Officer! Nor *'im.* 'E's me mate. It's 'im over theer as tha wants. It's 'im as 'as bin pinchin' me car..." and I point an accusing finger at Proper Car Thief.

Only a tinge embarrassed at his mistake, Sergeant releases his meaty grasp on purple-faced Peter's neck. In the ecstasy which comes after a rescue from the jaws of certain death, Peter slides fitfully down the shiny blue bonnet to land in a crumpled heap on the concrete floor.

"Oh, Fothergill," bellows Sergeant Bluebottle to the young PC not six inches from his shoulder.

"It i'n't this 'un. It's 'im over yonder. Wes'll 'ave ter see ter 'im - *Properly!*"

Now, this last word must have been some sort of Constabulary Code, for as soon as he hears it, PC Fothergill slips into "Apprehend Felon" mode. He darts over to Proper Car Thief who is now shaking and grovelling in the corner, the complete personification of Trouser-Filling Terror.

Echoing the style of his superior officer, Fothergill lets out a menacing growl: "Oh, so 'e likes riding in cars, does 'e?"

He grabs Car Thief by the scruff of his puny little neck and hauls his catch bodily and squirming in terror, towards the police vehicle.

Sergeant Bluebottle has nipped smartly across to the constabulary vehicle and deftly flicks open the rear door.

"Well, let's see if 'e likes ridin' in this un, then."

Junior PC grabs Car Thief by the seat of his scruffy brown trousers and flings him violently across the back seat of the police car. Arms flailing and thus unable to arrest his horizontal trajectory, his felonious head meets the opposite door of the vehicle with a leaden thud. We are all convinced that he has departed for the Great Car Park in the Sky.

Slamming the door on their prey, Sergeant Bluebottle rubs his hands gleefully. He turns to me and adopts an air of confidentiality. " 'E's a reight good copper, is Tommo, tha sees. 'E's awreight, is t'lad... burr 'e can't stand thieves. 'E 'ates 'em to buggery - as yer can see fo' yersens."

By now, I am beside myself with inner feelings of guilt and self-recrimination. This legal assault on Car Thief, his impending arrest and trial, and his undoubted separation from his wife and family at Her Majesty's Pleasure, is all down to *me*.

My inner voice is giving me a right good telling off as it scolds me in overdrive: "*He's a poor, pathetic weakling.*"

"... so 'e likes riding in cars, does 'e?"

"He's never had a chance in life to make his way. Your car isn't that valuable - only a bit of tin and a few nuts and bolts for getting around now and again. You could have let him go his way in peace, couldn't you? You nasty, selfish, vindictive sod..."

This inner conversation with myself is shattered by the boom of Sergeant Bluebottle's triumphant pronouncement.

"We're tekkin 'im down to t'nick. An we's'll charge 'im. Can you foller us an' mek a statement?"

Numbly, I agree, half-considering submitting a plea there and then to let Car Thief go. But Sergeant spins on his heel and makes for his vehicle, rubbing his hands and chortling joyfully with constabulary delight.

"Ee - Copped red-'anded. These are t'ones as tha dreams about, Tommo," and the pair make off with their prey still comatose in the back of their car. They speed down Peel Street onto Bradford Road and disappear in the direction of the Town Hall nick.

Heaving a great sigh of relief and ascertaining that all is well, Russell looks anxiously at his watch. He takes his leave along with Peter Hatton and they drive away into the night.

The silent, lonely gloom of the Bradford Road side-street engulfs me.

Ruefully and filled with remorse for my actions over the past half-hour, I make my way to my car for the drive to the Police Station in Dewsbury centre.

Imagine my dismay when I finally access the driver's seat.

After carefully fending off any contact between the gear-stick and my nether regions, I lower myself gingerly into the driver's seat.

There, lying on the floor under the steering-column, is a resplendent array of coloured wires, trailing across the rubber mat like kiddies' fun-time spaghetti. The ignition lock is hanging limply from the column, impotent and useless. And I am going nowhere in the immediate future.

"What do you do now," whines my inner voice. *"You know nothing about car electrics, do you, you clever bugger? So now you're stuck up Peel Street at midnight - without a paddle."*

And then the tone changes to one of admonishment: *"It serves you right for being so mean to poor, puny Car Thief. So get out of this mess if you can..."*

Gazing blankly at the array of wires, I begin to do some figuring out.

It hadn't appeared to me that Car Thief had been over-loaded in the brains department. Further to that, I figured, it was highly unlikely that he possessed a degree in Car Nicking:

Mr C.Thief   BSc Hons.(Oxon)   Vehicle Theft

But he *had* intended driving away in my car, so there must be a way of getting my old Viva to fire up sufficient life in order to transport me to the Police Station and Home.

Cautiously, I pick up the tangle of wires and notice two of them with bared ends. Having a penchant for gambling, and plucking up all my courage, I wager odds of 6-4 with my inner self that these two wires are those which will start the car. I lay a fifty pence piece on the seat beside me and vow that the winner takes all if I'm right.

Holding my breath and screwing my eyes tightly shut, I touch the two bare wires together. There is a vivid orange flash, the wires leap apart in my hands but the engine coughs into life. Saved by the ignition!

After pocketing my 50 pee winnings, I drive carefully through the silent midnight streets of Dewsbury to the Town Hall nick. I park up in the deserted side-street next to the Victorian master-piece which is an echo of times long gone, and enter through a side-door on Wakefield Road.

A sleep-logged Desk Sergeant ushers me into a stark, windowless interview room and I am given a cup of luke-warm tea. Left to my own devices, I look about me at the four grey walls which surround me, and I long for the green, green grass of home!

About twenty minutes later, Junior PC Fothergill enters the room with a large official-looking note-pad.

"Now, this won't take long, sir," he says, taking off his Bluebottle jacket and parking his nether region in the chair on the other side of the table. He licks the end of his pencil carefully, squares up the sheets of his note-pad and we begin my "statement".

PC Fothergill proceeds to question me about the entire incident. Slowly, painstakingly and deliberately, he writes down every single word I say, right down to the last syllable.

At 1.00am, I trail dejectedly out of the Town Hall side-door to hot-wire my vehicle and make my careful way home to Batley.

All the way along a silent, deserted Bradford Road and up Soothill Lane, I feel utterly wretched. I have ruined Car

Thief's whole life by shopping him and providing the authorities with a witnessed account of his activities which will surely hang him out to dry. If only I'd let him go, he might at this very moment be sitting with his family, a changed man because of my benificence.

I pictured him vowing to his little kiddies never to touch any *beastly* cars *ever* again.

"An' it's all thanks to that nice Mr Butler who gave me a second chance," I hear him say as he scans the "Situations Vacant" column in the Dewsbury Reporter.

But the reality was somewhat different.

At that very minute, he was banged up in a police cell down Dewsbury, nursing an egg-sized swelling in the cranium region. The only company he would have for the rest of the long night would be Sergeant Bluebottle and Junior PC Fothergill who would watch over him and attend to all his physical needs.

I almost shed a silent tear.

Yet again, I'd made an immediate judgement about my fellow human-beings without pausing to consider the effects. I'd jumped in hastily with both feet, failing to respond to the delicacy of the true situation.

Ah well, it was too late now...

I parked the car for the night and made my lonely way inside for a mug of very late-night/early morning cocoa.

And that, you might think, was that. Put the whole episode down to experience - one of Life's Little Lessons to be learned and inwardly digested.

As time passed, the incident receded in my mind...

Rehearsals for "Reluctant Heroes" took precedence over most things and mounting piles of exam papers began to demand my immediate attention. But then, one Friday evening some four months later, there is a bit of a salutary twist to the tale.

Sitting on the settee in our living-room, I was relaxing with my copy of the Dewsbury Reporter. Flicking idly through, I came across a report of recent court cases and their respective outcomes. One Kevin Ashley Humpleby, of no fixed address, had been found guilty of attempting to take and drive away a motor vehicle in Peel Street, Dewsbury.

"That was my car, " I announced plaintively to the four walls, and I read on.

During the hearing, the accused had admitted the said offence and asked for several others to be taken into consideration. These included several car thefts in Sheffield and Doncaster at about the same time; the stealing of cash from a local grocers' *and* the snatching of a pensioner's purse on Dewsbury Market a few weeks before.

His solicitor pleaded mitigating circumstances in that Humpleby, being a single man out of work, had no family to turn to for support in a time of crisis.

And to think I was going to let him off...

***

ONE OF  THE LADS

Bedraggled and wet-through, they crowded into the cardboard box which masqueraded as my Head of Year office at the far end of the school. They stood in front of me, all but one of them showing that nonchalant air of defiance. Five 14 year-old miscreants, dragged back in to school at 12.45pm in a big white police van.

Upon arrival in the wide, glass-fronted entrance hall, frantic efforts had been made by Head Office to get them out of sight a.s.a.p. before anybody could set eyes on them. Naughty boys brought in by West Yorkshire Constabulary half-way through the dinner hour was bad news indeed for the image of the school.

In the twinkling of an eye, it was ascertained which school year they belonged to and they were instructed to report to their Head of Year to explain themselves.

Another Shoddy Town tale unfolds...

He'd been to the College many times before, so it wasn't as if today was a new experience. Wednesday afternoon trips across town were now "an important part of his Upper School course". At least, that was what they had said at school when they sold him the idea on a balmy day in June, just before break, when everyone was itching to get outside.

But Tom Healey knew differently. They were occupying his time; preventing him from getting into mischief; ensuring his full attention at all times...

"And on Wednesday afternoons, you will be given a choice of activities, as shown in your Option Choice Booklets..."

There was a general rustle of bright green covers and a murmur of anticipation from the assembled gathering of Year 9 pupils..."but don't look at them now."

"Well what's tha given us 'em for?" thought Tom, but he complied with the instruction.

"There will be Housecraft Skills organised by Miss Middlemarch and Mrs Sweeney will run a Jewellery group. Mr Cowthorpe will offer Outdoor Pursuits and there will be two classes at DABTAC* - Office Skills and Bricklaying. Miss Fretwelle will be in charge of that group."

Well there was only one to go for!

Tom's dad had been a mill-hand at Wormalds and Walkers before he'd been made redundant and his mum cleaned at some big offices in town. Engineering was no good to Tom, so he plumped for Bricklaying. He'd heard there were some good jobs in the building trade from some of the lads off the estate who'd left school last year.

As it happened, Daz, Nupper, Wozzie and Bate had all opted for the same choice, knowing that it would be an afternoon out of school. Miss Fret couldn't control them anyway - they'd be able to do as they liked...

And so it had turned out: Bricklaying it was, down at the College.

Miss Fret would come down at 2.00 pm on the dot to

* Dewsbury and Batley Technical and Art College

"Link Course Classroom 3" to mark the register and to hastily make an apologetic exit, rarely to be seen again during the afternoon.

The lads went off to play at building walls, knocking them down again, mixing "compo" and throwing it at each other and at the Old Fogey in charge of the class.

They were able to pass wind liberally and use the foulest of language, escaping detection by giving false names and telling lies about their whereabouts at precise times. What did the teacher know? He was just some old git roped in from retirement to run the class. Week after dreary week, he repeated the same activities with monotonous regularity so it was inevitable that they would look for some excitement in the form of mischief, wasn't it?

Tom joined in with the mischief, but never in the wholehearted fashion of some of the others.

He always had a nagging doubt at the back of his mind that what they were doing was wrong. On occasions, he even felt sorry for the Old Fogey, but to abstain was impossible. He'd never live it down when they got back to school.

This was their eighth afternoon at the College now, so there was nothing new in preparing to shamble down the steep incline of Old Bank. They would soon cross town after racing round the Wednesday afternoon market stalls, and amble slowly up Halifax Road towards the imposing Victorian buildings of "The College". But for some reason, today was different ...

Bate had his arm in a pot after a fall from his bike; Wozzie's trainers were falling to pieces and his feet were soaking wet; Nupper had no cigs; Daz was waxing lyrical about how he'd had his hand up Karen Cropper's blouse during a Biology lesson that morning.

So there was nothing new there, thought Tom.

But there *was* an atmosphere - a feeling that he couldn't put words to; a sense of something in the air...

The group of lads turned the corner outside the school gates, paused at the top of the steep incline and selected a grassy bank on which to sit and enjoy their temporary freedom.

They gazed out at the vast panorama of Dewsbury which lay below them, from the railway yard on the left, the Town Hall in the centre, to DABTAC on the right. The Leeds and Wakefield Road cuttings sliced their diesel-ridden swathes around the imposing Victorian Town Hall as the Wednesday afternoon traffic hummed and buzzed its way towards Flushdyke and Shaw Cross.

Such an impressive view of a Shoddy Town at work left the lads unimpressed and they pooled resources for a smoke.

Ruefully, Tom parted company with a tab-end he'd been saving so that Nupper could join in the ritual. As a result of his injured arm, Bate subjected himself to a frantic search through his pockets for a match, and soon the lads were enveloped in a cloud of friendly smoke.

"Hey, It's a bad un is this, Healey! Where did yer gerrit?" scorned Nupper.

"What tha complainin' about," replied Tom, with like scorn. "Tha gorrit fer nowt, din't yer?"

"Shurrup thee," shouted Bate, "else Ahs'll dong thi wi' me pot." He brandished his arm above his head after jerking it out of the sling.

The wrist was encased in a once-white plaster, covered now in signatures, messages of love, drawings of willies and several designed-to-shock obscenities. It had provided a useful excuse for missing PE over the weeks, and he'd even kidded Miss Fret that he wrote left-handed, so he'd skipped RE too.

"I'm bloody sick of this Bricklayin' though," whined Wozzie, the voice of doom and gloom.

"All we do is sit and watch yon feller layin' bricks. I thought we was gunna have a go ussens, like. I wish I'd done chuffin' needlework now." Tom silently agreed as they began the saunter down the hill.

The feeling of the impending gloom of the afternoon seemed to pervade the whole group as they reached the bottom of the steep slope to be swallowed up in the noise and clamour of the town.

The mighty 42 horse-power diesel engines of the great trailer lorries toiled in low gear up the steep incline towards the big roundabout at Flushdyke. Their fearsome roar carved a sonic route up the main road on the way to the motorway and the far corners of England. The noise deafened the OAP's who shambled their arduous ways to the Market and the shops, rattling teeth in heads.

Now, however, there was a temporary lift from the gloomy atmosphere because it was time for some "fun".

As the juggernauts toiled past, you could rush up to any Old Git [whose hearing wasn't so good anyway] and shout the filthiest of swear-words at him. Sometimes he would smile and say "Yes, lad, tha'r reight", but more often than not it would be a cursory "Cheeky young bugger".

Male or female, they hadn't a clue what you'd shouted. Great fun, because you knew you wouldn't get caught, and anyway, they couldn't prove you'd actually said anything. Tom joined in the "fun", but always felt pangs of guilt - one of these old gits could have been his Grandad, and he'd wouldn't have dared to tell *him* to shove a banana up his arse or to go and "play wi' issen".

Twenty or so hilarious minutes later, the lads were weaving their way through the Wednesday afternoon market shoppers.

They bumped into Old Gits and young women with little tots and were cursed for it. They tapped on shop-windows to irritate shop-keepers and ran off. They played tag on the steps of the Playhouse until a bobby rounded the corner of Foundry Street and gave them a meaningful stare. So at last there was nothing for it but to ascend the hill and approach the smoke-blackened towers of the College.

They stopped for a last fag at the pelican crossing and shouted invitations to some girls who were making for the Office Skills class. Then, like soldiers carrying out a drill order, they nipped their cigarettes and prepared to trudge inside.

Anger was mounting - anger at the thought of having to pass the next two hours watching an Old Fart laying bricks. The only relief was in the fact that this was a shared anger - unreleasable but shared, and this made it somehow easier to bear. Tom led the way in through the arched doorway.

It was if Nupper voiced all their thoughts at once - almost as if he'd read their minds:

"Hey - do you think they'd miss us if we buggered off?"

They all paused, ground to a halt, and considered the question. " 'Course they would," said Wozzie. "We've to gerrus register marked, 'aven't we? An' they look at 'em back at school, tha knows. 'Epworth'd gerrus in t'mornin'"

"Gerraway, man!" This was Bate, who had a gleam in his eye. "We could gerrus register marked 'ere and then piss off. Miss Fret weeant miss us. Anyroad, she's in t'staffroom most o' t' time, suppin' coffee."

"An' Ah'm not stoppin' and listenin' to yond old fart talkin' about cement-mixers and setting up corners again. Ah'm off when we've done t'registers. Who else?" This was Nupper, the defiant one.

Gradually, the idea appealed to them all, but indecision enveloped Tom.

He didn't like trouble in any shape or form and usually did his level best to avoid it. In his mind's eye he saw the Deputy Head - old Hepworth - brandishing a Thursday morning cane. He swallowed hard.

"Ah'm not nicking off. Tha'r mad - tha'll get stick tomorrer mornin'"

"And tha'r bloody yeller, 'Ealey," observed Nupper.

"Ah'm not! Ah've got sense, that's all."

"Aw, come on, Tom. It's nobbut a bit o' fun. Nobody'll

miss us - wes'll be safe as 'ouses," enthused Daz. He'd been persuaded by Nupper as he succumbed to the adolescent threat of being called "yeller".

"We can go to Caddy's, then we'll be off o' t'streets," added Wozzie. "Besides, it's ter cowd fer owt else."

Tom's resolve was beginning to falter. He hated the idea of the bricklaying class as much as any of them. Besides which, he still had a few pence left from last week's "spend". Caddy's was warm and the ice-cream they served was world famous for its flavour. His resolve collapsed:

"Reight then - Ah'm off an' all." As soon as the words left his lips, he realised what that feeling was that he had experienced not half an hour ago.

Inside, he had known that there was something in the air - a sense of anticipation, of waiting for something out of the ordinary to happen. But he lacked the words to express it.

His heart had leapt when he said the words. A sense of excitement hit him like a blow in the gut.

He hadn't felt like this since his Junior school days, when they'd been discovered pinching apples from Hardcastle's orchard on the way home. They'd sprinted all the way down Pildacre Lane and into Wozzie's garden shed on Cedar Road where they'd holed up for at least two hours...

With the decision made and unanimously agreed, the group ambled down the long, neon-lit tiled Victorian corridor. They sauntered into a dingy classroom with a heavy, panelled door and a high echo-chamber ceiling, where Miss Fretwelle, a pleasant, grey-haired, well-meaning old body [only lately recruited to the teaching profession] was at the desk, surrounded by a horde of boisterous adolescents, in most respects resembling a troupe of chattering monkeys.

"Ah'm 'ere, miss!"

"Number twenty-two, miss!"

"Miss, can we go now?"

"Number one, miss! Top o' t'sheet."

"Miss, can Ah go to t'toilet?"

"Miss, Ah'm 'ere!"

"Are yer 'ell as like."

"Ah bloody am!"

"Poor old Miss Fret," thought Tom. *"She's helpless and useless and we're not making it easy for her."*

The group of lads remained at the back of the room, chatting amongst themselves and generally ignoring the registration process. "Clayton," called a feeble voice from the middle of the crowd.

"Yes miss," returned Bate

"Nutting."

"Present, miss." That was Nupper, pretending politeness, to ensure recognition.

"Healey."

" 'Ere, miss," called Tom, a lump of guilt in his throat.

At last, the register was complete. The noise level had remained constant throughout, and it was time for Miss Fret to make her weekly supplication to the assembled gathering of monkeys: "Now go to your classes, and remember ..."

Her ageing, feeble voice, asking for good behaviour and consideration for others was lost in the rush out of the door.

Out on the corridor, carefully and craftily, the group of lads sidled their way towards Construction Workshop B.

Glancing over their shoulders, they noticed Miss Fret come out of the classroom which they had just left, pause for a moment to look both ways, Highway Code fashion, and finally turn away from them to waddle off in the direction of the Staff Room. She'd be no doubt relishing the thought of spending the next hour or so warming her big fat bum in a cosy armchair.

"That's 'er out o' t'way," hissed Nupper.

The rest was easy.

Instead of ascending the central staircase, they turned left off the main corridor and into the toilets. They noticed, briefly, how different it was from school. There were no toilet rolls on the floor or down the pans; there wasn't the putrifying stench of unflushed WC's and there was an absence of smoking boys occupying the cubicles. The whole place smelled clean and cared-for.

A ten minute wait was all that was necessary to ensure quiet corridors occupied by an occasional passing student and a group of caretakers discussing the likely outcome of the 2.45 Handicap Chase at Doncaster.

As the lads descended the steps onto the main road, a cold, damp drizzle began to fall...

Ambling down towards the town-centre, Tom shook off

the last vestiges of a guilt feeling which had steadily decreased in proportion to their distance away from the College. They were safe now, weren't they? The register had been marked, hadn't it? Miss Fret would be half way through her second coffee by now, wouldn't she? All the facts seemed to fit neatly into a completed jigsaw of tidy events.

"Where we off, then?" he asked Nupper, cheerfully.

"Caddy's, Ah reckon. It's ter bloody wet to stop out."

After general agreement, they made their wary way through the busy, market-day streets.

They sneaked past The Little Saddle where a piano was playing and Wozzie's Dad might be enjoying a lunch-time pint. They sidled off down the dark, cobbled alley, all the while casting furtive glances over their shoulders. Finally they walked round the back, bold as brass, into the warm and welcoming Espresso atmosphere of the Italian ice-cream parlour...

An hour later, they were leaving at pace, hotly pursued by the unforgettable figure of Luigi Carrera and a mixture of Italian invective and Yorkshire dialect:

"Getta da Hellouta here, you leetle fookers. You ruin-a ma tables and break-a da coop. I make-a you pay for this in a real-a brass. You no coom back 'ere - I no want-a you back 'ere, or I tell your-a father. Booger off. I tell-a your teacher an' you get a-fookin stick tomorra. Who's-a gonna pay for this breaking?"

"Gerron wi' yer, yer fat Eytie get," shouted Nupper as they rounded the safety of the corner, out of sight.

"Yer daft twat, Bate! What did yer do that for?"

"Ah wor only seein' if t'ash-tray would spin on its end," explained Bate. "It wor cracked, anyroad."

"So now what we gunner do," inquired Tom, turning up his collar as feeble protection against the cold, soaking drizzle. He was beginning to regret leaving the Building class - at least it was warm there.

"Easy," said a confident Nupper. "There's loads o' places we can go to keep warm - Boots, t'Co-op, t'Bon-Bon. " He rattled off a list of walk-round stores and cafes. "They're all good for half an hour, to keep aht o' t'cowd." Almost by common consent, the lads made soldier-like for Boots the Chemist and marched in.

The place was a clamour of market-day bodies - pushing, heaving, sighing and shoving - but very few shopping. Just like the lads, the majority were in there for the warmth.

"Ey, lerrus 'ave a game o' summat," enthused Wozzie. They all thought that this was an admirable suggestion, and Bate with his pot was elected to be "it" in a game of tag.

Like infant school urchins, they chased up and down the crowded aisles, crashing past middle-aged women and their burdensome shopping-bags and bashing frightened young shop-assistants out of the way.

The real "skill" of the game was to disguise the fact that they were, in reality, playing a kiddies' game, so when the pin-striped, bespectacled manager hove-to on the horizon, there was an immediate behaviour transformation:

Change down to bottom gear, walk slowly and serenely past him, looking for all the world like an innocent child, sent down town on an errand for an ageing Granny.

When he's passed by, back into overdrive, hurtling up and down the rows of sickly smelling soaps and shampoos.

Rapidly engage reverse when a young trainee pin-stripe cuts short one of Daz's superb sprints and demands his name and address.

Moments later, after a quick round-up on the pavement, they were once again seeking refuge from the weather.

With a crafty glint in his eye, Nupper asked: "Oh - 'ave any of yer bin in Woollies lately?"

Bate, with a similar glint, said that he had and that it had been "real". Without realising what that glint signified, Tom needed no urging to join in - he was still cold and wet: "Well come on then. What we waitin' for? Let's go."

Carried off by Nupper's enthusiasm for the visit to Woollies, Tom was still trying to figure out the meaning behind those remarks as they entered the store through the dark oak-and-glass panelled doors. He knew there was something important in visiting Woolworths' - he could tell by their tone. But he had no idea what it was.

Nupper's furtive whisper to Bate reinforced his feelings of anticipation and excitement, but he didn't know why as he followed the others into the electric warmth of the store.

Daz, Nupper, Wozzie and Bate paused for the merest moment at the entrance and looked round.

Perfect! Plenty of shoppers filled the aisles, all concentrating on the available bargains, far too busy to notice a group of five adolescent schoolboys.

Slowly, and with a care of movement Tom had not noticed before, Nupper set off. He wandered nonchalantly past the open display counters, stopping here and there to pick up and inspect various articles. A light-plug; [He shook his head and replaced it.]; a paint-brush [again the shake of the head]; a screw-driver [this time, an appreciative nod].

Tom looked round.

All the lads were following Nupper's lead - picking up an article, turning it over in their hands, inspecting, shaking their heads and returning said article to the counter.

Now, there didn't appear to be a great deal of fun to be had out of such activitiy, but Tom joined in, just so that he might become part of the proceedings. After a while, he began to feel silly. So it was time to move on.

He looked over his shoulder and noticed that Daz and Bate had now stopped playing the game and had both adopted relaxed but watchful poses, leaning against a nearby pillar. He looked round for Nupper.

Just as Tom's glance fell on him, the last-named's hand swept from the sweet counter to his side in a smooth, magician-like movement, and left its illicit deposit in his jacket pocket. This occurred three times in as many seconds, before Nupper the Thief moved off to join Daz and Bate.

At this point of suspended animation, Tom realised just exactly what it was that had captured his attention. He admired the skill with which the various articles were being taken and he admired the organization of the whole affair; but he deplored the fact that this was stealing and he was frightened of it. He wanted none of this, so he turned to go. If he walked slowly, he would arrive at the shop for his paper-round at the usual time and no-one would know that he had missed school.

"Oh, Healey....." He was stopped in his tracks by Nupper's hissed call.

"Come on, we're off down to t'bottom end."

A moment of decision: Tom didn't want to be left out. He didn't want the scorn which would undoubtedly follow at morning break tomorrow if he were to leave now. He wanted to be the same as the others, but he knew it was wrong.

"There's a load o' stuff down 'ere that we can sell at school tomorrer - just mek sure as tha dun't get caught, that's all," said Nupper, leading the lads down a central aisle. "Ah 'aven't seen thee doin' owt, Healey. What's up - yeller? Chicken?"

The old taunt.

But Tom wasn't going to appear frightened, even if he was shaking with fear.

" 'Aven't seen owt as Ah want, yet," he said, as casually as he could under the circumstances, but his hand had now been forced. He wanted to be one of the lads, but there was a strong voice from his conscience telling him that he didn't like trouble and to avoid it. The voice was soon drowned out as the desire to be accepted welled up.

"Reight," he said. "Watch this!"

He looked round to check that the coast was clear and that Nupper was 'on duty'?, leaning against a pillar with a watchful eye on things.

"Reight."

A rush of excitement mixed up with many other emotions surged up and an invisible hand pushed him further and further forward to the edge of the counter. His heart pounded and throbbed in his ears as he picked up a small torch and secreted it away in his pocket.

He looked up.

Nupper and the others were all nodding appreciatively and smiling grimly whilst watching out for "trouble". The rush seized him again. He went for another torch to sell at school tomorrow.

This time, he dwelt a while on the inspection, for the benefit of his "audience" behind him, before the furtive slide into the pocket.

"And what the bloody hell do you think you're doing?"

A heavy hand fell on Tom's shoulder. He whipped round to be faced by the serge-blue of the policeman's uniform.

The others had gone - nowhere to be seen...

The cane stung his hands on Thursday morning, but his mother's tears stung his conscience on Wednesday night.

***

DINNER TIME

I've always been a bit wary of people who use the word "lunch" when referring to their mid-day meal.

For me, and all the Shoddy Town folk with whom it has been my privilege to work for the last forty-odd years, that mid-day repast was always referred to as "mi dinner". Nowadays, however, it seems to have undergone an identity change.

For one thing, it goes by another name. And for another, it consists of nothing more satisfying than a bit of bread with a foreign-sounding name and a very wholesome drink of fruit juice. These portable items of nourishment are deliberately chosen so that they can be consumed on foot.

In the 1960's Shoddy Towns, we called it "dinner" and we always undertook its consumption at around twelve o'clock, mid-day. That's when the factory buzzer sounded, or the foreman on your particular job called it all off for an hour or so, and you got to relax those aching limbs for a while...

My very first experience of the workaday dinner-time event occurred while I was working at P&C Garnett's, Textile Machine Makers, in Cleckheaton around 1961.

At the tender age of sixteen, I'd rapidly acquired the skill of grinding spikes for Mudrick rollers, of bagging them up in 500 lots and of clocking a card to indicate the time taken. Any officially allowed intermission in such tedious work was always gratefully received, so I soon fell into the habit of pacing out my day according to the clock and the breaks which it allowed.

Ten to nine in the morning heralded a ten minute repast called "breakfast". Twelve o'clock mid-day brought the welcome relief of one hour's respite for "mi dinner". And that was it - breaks were over for the day. Work began again at 1.00pm and there were no more official gaps in your day's toil until the heart-felt relief of the five o'clock buzzer and clocking off.

But dinner-time was a welcome sixty minutes' respite.

Now at the time, my Dad was the P&C Garnett's foundry manager and he was still a slave to routine. This meant that he liked to get home every day for his dinner, so I was expected to follow suit.

With the dying notes of the mid-day buzzer still throbbing on the post-meridian air, he would pull up in his green Rover 2000 status symbol adjacent to the time-clock. I would clock off at 12.00pm precisely, [we were allowed five minutes in which to wash our hands and prepare for the hundred yard sprint to the clock], and at two minutes past, The Old Boy and I would be gliding serenely up Stone Street, salivating expectantly.

Meanwhile, back home in Liversedge, Mum would have a dinner of Gargantuan proportions ready for our disposal.

Mountains of mashed potatoes, huge slices of rich steak pie to be followed by an extremely tasty apple sponge and gallons of thick, creamy custard.

At about ten past twelve, the workers would arrive.

The green Rover glides to a purring halt in the driveway.

The Foundry Manager and his First Born exit the vehicle at the speed of light and enter the kitchen. We take our places, grab our eating-irons and raise them aloft.

With a perfect sense of timing, Mother deftly slides two heaped plates in the vacant spaces and the victual ritual begins.

By 12.37pm, both courses have been consumed, we workers are indulging in our post-prandial cups of tea and Wild Woodbines, while Mum sets about the washing-up. Her mind is already turning to thoughts of "what to give them for their tea..."

At 12.50pm, the workers are once more on the road to Cleckheaton, relishing the thought of another afternoon of daily travail without a break.

After clocking my card, I take up station behind my six-inch grinding-wheel, ready for four hours' worth of Mudrick spikes.

By 2.30pm, I begin to feel the effects of that huge intake of food.

My belly feels as though it is about to slip out of the bottoms of my blue engineer's overalls, such is its leaden weight, and I keep rubbing my lower gut in order to check its current position. In the heat of the machine-shop, with its hundreds of lathes, milling machines and electric motors, I have all on to keep my eyes open and to fight off post-prandial slumber.

In my mind's eye, I see visions of a comfortable settee on which to sprag myself out, and my eyelids begin to droop wistfully. The electric whirring of the machines becomes a restful hum and my eyes glaze over. My shoulders droop, my head sags forward and I fancy I can hear the soft twittering of larks in a clear blue sky...

I am wrenched back to reality at the screech of the small grinding wheel which is by now but three inches away from my sleep-logged nose. Yanking back a half-ground spike and averting injury of First Aid proportions, I jerk myself back to full height in front of my work station.

I flex my eyebrows in the effort to stay awake.

Desperately, I look round to see if anybody has spotted my near-lapse into the land of Nod, but all the other machinists are busy about their workaday tasks. If I fell asleep on the job, I would never live it down, to say nothing of what my Dad would say or do.

Vowing to have a word with Mum about the quantity [but not the quality] of the mid-day dinner, I return to sharpening spikes with one eye on the clock.

In just two hours and twenty-five minutes, I shall be consuming yet another huge intake of nourishment, but this time it will be called "mi tea"...

So it was almost inevitable that eventually, I would beg my Dad to allow me to stay at work for "mi dinner".

I could enjoy the company of my mates and a kick-about in the yard, couldn't I? More importantly, I might be able to scale down the mid-day intake of nourishment, so that I would make it through the afternoon without falling asleep. Thankfully, he agreed, so at that point in my working career, I came to sample the delights of the bacon 'n' egg tea-cake.

The said sandwich was a culinary delight on offer for a shilling at the shop at the top of Stone Street.

At about 11.30am on the day you'd decided to opt for your bob's worth of taste sensation, Victor the Pole would approach you at your work station.

Victor was a swarthy, East European who'd ended up in the Heavy Woollen District after the war. He was one of the labourers in the machine-shop but, in addition to that heavy responsibility, he had assumed the role of "shop-man" for us all.

He stands before me now, smiling enquiringly across the motor of the heavy milling machine next to my grinding-wheel.

"Arah yoo 'avin' owt terdayah, owdah ahladah, pleasah," he asks politely.

"Aye, Victor! Bacon 'n' egg tea-cake." I order eagerly and proffer my bright, shiny shilling.

Thirty minutes later, the welcome strains of the twelve o'clock buzzer have hardly died away as Victor comes trotting down the centre aisle of heavy machinery. In his wicker basket, he carries his culinary treasures of alimentary delights which he proceeds to lay out on top of Jack Howgate's planing table.

We grab our dinners and return to make-shift seats beside our machines.

For the first time, I am about to sample the delights of my bacon 'n' egg dinner. My mouth juices flow in rivers down my drooling chops. My mandibles open to maximum in order to accommodate the four-inch width of the tea-cake and its contents. With anticipatory relish, I snap my incisors shut.

A soft, golden spurt of egg-yolk shoots from the sides

of the tea-cake, defies gravity for a fleeting moment and then cascades in a greasy film down the sleeve of my overalls. The best part of my dinner has departed, undigested, down my arm.

As a result, my form in the ensuing dinner-time kick-about was abysmal, and I failed to score.

Determined to savour the *complete* delights of a bacon 'n' egg tea-cake, however, I am undaunted.

The following day [and for many days thereafter], I place a repeat order with Victor the Pole, each time hoping that the egg is not a soft, gooey affair. On several occasions, I am disappointed, as I manage to spray egg-yolk to all four corners of my work-place.

Thin, yellow trickles of egg-yolk flow down the guards on my machine. My Daily Mirror racing page is unreadable under a yellow-slime. Bespectacled Tommy Fanning, the miller of the Mudrick spikes sitting opposite me, once had to wash off his glasses under the tap. But sometimes, the entire egg-white and all, would splurt out of the far end of my tea- cake and land defiantly on my working-boot which was covered in machine-shop oil and dross.

On the very last occasion I remember, my shilling's worth of culinary pleasure shot from its warm, snug tea-cake and skated along the greasy floor under my machine. Crawling around to retrieve it, I considered re-instating it between the slices of my bread, but when I saw the bits of metal turnings and swarf which had lodged in the yolk, I kicked it away into the dark recesses of the machine-bed.

For all I know, it's still there, hard and inedible, waiting for some Shoddy Town mouse to pass by and devour it.

Not long after that, I forsook my dinner-time footballing mates and the gastronomic delights of the corner shop to return to my previous dinner-time practice. I went home at 12.02pm with my Dad in his Rover 2000, older and much wiser...

A few years later, during my student days, I served my dinner-time apprenticeship as a labourer at John Crosslands, a building firm in Hightown.

I enjoyed wielding a pick and shovel at Burnley's Gomersal Mill where Crosslands were permanently based. There's a long, red-brick building on the left, about two hundred yards from the once-thriving mill's gates. The two storey edifice now bears the logo "Spen Valley Scouring" and its present-day purpose in life is to serve as the Greasy Wool Warehouse. I vividly remember joining a gang of six or seven huge men one summer's morning in 1964, to dig out the foundations for its construction.

It was an integral part of my education to accompany those jolly men who could have eaten me for breakfast as we set off from our builder's cabin at a distant corner of the thriving mill complex. With our picks and shovels over our shoulders we whistle while we walk to the site of our daily toil.

Our first task was to break out concrete with a compressor and a jack-hammer. Once the dark-brown of Mother Earth had been exposed, we set to and dug out a trench of perhaps 30 yards in length. We worked one behind the other, in lines reminiscent of Victorian navvies, and, at the close of every working day, it was a joy to behold the "footings" gradually deepening and lengthening as the days went by.

But of course, the real education was delivered during the 12 o'clock dinner-times.

I'd long since abandoned the trip home for one of my Mum's Gargantuan mid-day feasts. Now, I was my own man with my *own* *snap-tin which had been carefully prepared the night before..

I see it now, with its hinged green lid, thin metal body and its treasure trove of dinner-time goodies: Two thickly buttered Marmite sandwiches and a Kit-Kat lie wrapped clumsily in grease-proof paper. A brown envelope containing half-a-dozen teaspoonfuls of sugar nestles in one corner of the metal tin. In the other, jammed up against the grease- proof paper, its mate, containing three heaped spoonfuls of PG Tips. And between them, an old TCP bottle full of milk. Enough to keep you going for the next three or four hours.

As soon as Joe Dickinson, our site foreman gave the signal, we would down tools in the trench, climb out and hare off for the distant cabin. About five minutes before, old, grey-haired George Wilkinson, whose advancing age meant that he was best suited to domestic cabin duties, would have boiled the kettle on a rusty gas ring and poured the scalding contents on to our "mashings". By the time we arrived, our tea would just have reached drinkable temperature.

Scrabble for your snap-tin which had lain undisturbed on the cabin table since the ten to nine breakfast time that morning; pour copious quantities of sugar into your pot of steaming tea; unfold the Daily Mirror from your jacket pocket and settle down to listen to the cheerful banter.

* snap   lunch-time sandwiches, hastily prepared that
          morning. Sometimes referred to as "jock"

Such dinner-times were the stuff of any young man's educational legend. There would always be some incident of note to recount and laugh about, to keep you amused through the approaching long afternoon of hot toil.

Like that time when old George had been detailed to a mid-morning task of replenishing the dumper-truck's filler-can with diesel fuel.

He'd decided to avail himself of the flat space afforded him by the cabin's rickety old table-top, so he stood the portable, one gallon filler-can upright on the table and went outside for its blue, five gallon counterpart.

Heaving and straining, George only just managed to lift the larger can up onto the table. With increasing physical anguish, he struggled to lift the heavier can and aim a generous flow of diesel-fuel down the narrow neck of the filler-can. His arms trembled and quivered with the effort of it all as copious quantities of the pink, odorous liquid slopped out onto the table.

In tiny rivulets, it flowed around the several snap-tins which had been placed there and, as George's strength began to flag, it even slopped into the open lids of one or two of them...

Twelve o'clock arrives. Picks and shovels are joyfully abandoned in the bottom of the trench and we race round to the cabin for our dinner-time period of Rest and Refreshment. Minutes later, we enter the dilapidated shack, and our pots of tea are ready on the table, steaming and waiting. We begin the daily scrabble for our victuals.

"What's that f....... smell," enquires Big Ned, sniffing the cabin air like a bloodhound on the scent of a trail.

"Why are mi sarnies sooakin' wet," demands Bert Lockwood as he presses a filthy thumb into the white bread of his tea-cake.

I join in the inquisition. "What's all this slop in t' bottom o' mi snap-tin?"

George swallows hard. He is casting a wary eye over Big Ned's huge tattooed forearms and noticing the anvil-like qualities of Bert Lockwood's fists.

George mumbles, almost inaudibly, in a corner: "Ah think someone must 'a' spilt some diesel, or summat," and we all readily agree.

We decide to take our refreshment alfresco to escape the over-powering diesel-fumes which linger in the rafters of the unventilated cabin. There is an unusual silence as we sit on the floor, backs to the cabin's wooden wall, munching our mid-day sustenance.

After about five minutes' munching, Bert breaks the silence. "Ah'm bahna spayk to t'wife abaht these f...... tea-cakes," he whines. "They're f...... rammy. She'll 'a' ter change bakers."

George remains silent, keeping shtumm.

Big Ned screws up his mighty nose and slings a half-devoured sandwich across the yard. "An' Ahs'll 'a' ter change butchers, an' all. This mayt must be off."

Still no word from George.

Of the gang, I seem to have escaped lightly.

Today, my sarnies are of the banana variety, with a little added sugar. The natural pungency of the fruit-filling masks the smell and taste of diesel so I gulp them down in a trice. In a few minutes, I am deep into today's perusal of the racing pages in my Daily Mirror.

A silence falls on the gang.

After about twenty minutes, we all begin to pass wind at rapidly increasing intervals, piercing the peace of the dinner-time rest period with bugle blasts of varying lengths and pitch. Ned has to go for a drink of water: "Ter wesh t'taste o' yon rammy mayt at'n mi gob."

In no time at all, the stipulated half-hour dinner-time passes and Site Foreman Joe Dickinson comes out of his cabin, yawning and stretching. He purposefully dons his flat cap and rubs his hands - a signal to us all that our next four hours of toil is beckoning.

Old George heaves a sigh of relief as the digging gang departs round the corner of the mill building and out of sight for the rest of the shift. Not one of us has cottoned on to the fact that the savoury taste of our mid-day victuals has been severely infected with a gallon or two of pink, diesel fuel.

We amble slowly towards our trench, our walk punctuated by the cacophanous musical accompaniment of several navvies passing wind.

Later, at about three o'clock in the high heat of the afternoon, we began to feel the effects of a diesel-soaked dinner. One by one, we stop swinging our picks, lean on our shovels and discuss the current state of our common constitutions.

All our faces have erupted in identical red blotches. Stomach pains double us up until the welcome relief of passing wind. The rate at which this last phenomenon takes place has increased steadily over the last hour or so and it is now occurring, throughout the digging gang, at very rapid and regular intervals.

Such gaseous exchanges with the atmosphere are of an amazing sonic quality. At each blast, the office lasses in the adjacent building leap from their typewriters in a mad panic as if the fire siren has sounded. We all loosen our waist-belts as our stomachs swell up like party balloons.

But this was a labouring gang wasn't it? We shrugged our shoulders and assigned our current state of health to the unusually hot weather.

Our excavations continued throughout the afternoon to a background accompaniment of various bodily noises, until at last, five o'clock arrives and heralds the end of our day's toil. The walk back to the cabin is a very tuneful affair as we punctuate our stroll with a variety of gaseous emissions.

Leaning on the wall at the bus-stop at Gomersal Hill Top, I contemplate my impending journey home aboard a crowded bus. The free abandon of passing wind, afforded me by membership of a gang of navvies, would disappear for the next half-hour or so as the big, blue Number 63 bus [Bradford-Mirfield] trundles along its circuitous route through Cleckheaton, Littletown and Liversedge.

I alight at the Bar House with excruciating pains in my lower gut and pass wind in an ecstasy of relief...

The following bright morning, to Old George's evident delight, we all arrive, bright eyed and bushy tailed, for another day's toil. However, across each man's chin, yesterday's facial skin rash has erupted into a swathe of spots, but our gaseous complaint seems to have subsided amongst us all. We puzzle the morning away, in vain trying to establish why it is that we have all experienced the same physical symptoms.

Still puzzled at dinner time, we show no other ill-effects from yesterday's consumption. Old George heaves another sigh of relief as we down our snap and enjoy the banter of yet one more mid-day break.

No reference is made to yesterday's spillage as we munch our way through another half hour, and by the end of the stipulated break, the entire incident has passed into the misty clouds of time-gone-by.

Yet, even today, forty years on, I marvel inwardly at the way our digestive systems processed that pink, volatile fluid which prompted great black clouds of noxious fumes to billow from the dumper's exhaust pipe...

Another memorable workaday dinner time occurred not at a factory or building site in the Heavy Woollen District, but in a car park at Malham in the summer of 1967.

By now, I'm a fully fledged and experienced teacher of one year's standing, and my colleague, Selwyn Davey has recruited my services during the long school holiday. Selwyn, a dapper, bespectacled Welshman of many years educational experience, was in charge of the ethnic minorities group at Batley High School. It was his responsibility to oversee the "integration" into the English educational system of about fifty or so Asian lads.

In those days, such lads, who had had little experience of English school life, were educated separately from the rest of the school. From their induction up until they had acquired sufficient language skills to cope in the rough and tumble of the "main stream", they were taught in special groups. In classrooms on the lower floor, these lads had their own teachers who worked alongside one or two appointed Asian teachers to assist with language problems when they occurred.

One such assistant was Mr Shah. It was Selwyn's job to plan the educational diet and to drive it forward. It was the impeccably-dressed, meticulously polite Mr Shah who oiled the linguistic wheels.

During that summer holiday of 1967, Selwyn had organised some extra curricular activities for the group of lads in his charge. One such activity was a day trip to the Dales, and Yours Truly had been recruited, on a paid basis, to assist the group. Our ultimate objective was a walk to Malham Tarn, after taking our dinner-time break in the village car park.

The night before the trip, recalling my days at Burnley's Mill, I'd dug out my old snap-tin and filled it to capacity.

A variety of sandwiches lay across the bottom of the tin - some banana, some egg and some ham - and there were several Kit Kats and a packet or two of crisps. After all, this wasn't the "snap" of a full-time navvy with an afternoon's physical toil to come. No, I was a "professional" person now, so that meant a mid-day meal of some substance.

We board our hired coach at nine o'clock on a bright summer morning. Fifty lads, three teachers and Mr Shah who will be in charge of linguistic matters. Our day-trip charabanc glides through Batley filled with the excited chatter of the lads as they take note of the geographical locations through which we pass.

We trundle through Birstall Smithies and out onto the

main road to Bradford. As we negotiate the roundabout beside the West Riding Fire Station, Iftikhar Patel is anxious to display both his geographical and linguistic talents.

Pointing enthusiastically to a road-sign, he booms: "Oh, sir, look here! Brick-en-shaw," and he nods towards the side of the road.

In best teacher-mode, I correct him. "We say Birkenshaw, Iftikhar.

"Oh yes, sir Brickenshaw. Yes, sir." And he grins a toothy grin.

"What's he going to make of Bowling Old Lane, Laisterdyke or Little Germany when we get to Bradford," I ask myself. I move to another seat to avoid Iftikhar's inevitable future enquiries.

Not long after that, we have swept through many Dales villages, I have managed to avoid any impromptu pronunciation lessons, and we alight in the car park of a picturesque Malham village. Fifty Batley lads, along with their minders, settle down for dinner.

Adhering closely to Selwyn's instructions back at school a couple of days ago, the lads have all remembered their snap-tins and lunch-time goodies. In a hubbub of chatter, they descend upon the picnic area seats and set about their intake of oriental fare.

After a tour of inspection, during which we ask many questions as to the nature of various foodstuffs, we four adults find a seat some distance away from the chattering horde. With a relaxed sigh, we turn to our own snap-tins and access the contents thereof.

I remember looking up towards Malham Cove, relishing the savoury delights of a ham sandwich and the feeling of contentment which washed over me. There weren't many jobs on offer which would allow you the luxury of a day's paid labour in such idyllic surroundings.

Lost in such philosophical rêverie, I look across at Mr Shah. He is not eating.

In fact, he does not have a snap-tin in which to delve for his dinner. He sits, at some distance from Selwyn and I, gazing into the wide blue yonder.

With a feeling of some guilt at not noticing his plight, I approach my professional colleague. "Mr Shah," I mumble. "I ...er...notice..that, er... you're not....That is to say, you haven't anything to ...er...eat."

"I'm so sorry, Mr Bootler. I forget to bring any nourishment for this day. Even though Mr Davey tells me what to do and passes instructions at school. I am very forgettable, you know..."

Catching on to his predicament fairly swiftly, I am overcome with a rush of bountiful generosity. "Oh, you've forgotten to bring your snap, have you. Well, here, you can have some of mine."

I proffer the contents of my old snap-tin at arms length, and Mr Shah peers doubtfully at the contents.

"You very kind man, Mr Bootler. I am bit of a hunger, myself. May I take just one single sarnie?"

"Of course," I reply and shove the tin further under Mr Shah's scrutinizing gaze. "Help yourself."

Gratefully, Mr Shah acknowledges my personal sacrifice.

"Oh thank you so much, Mr Bootler. You are very good person."

He pauses and raises a doubtful eyebrow.

"Just one thing. Before I take my single sarnie, I must question: It is not pig, is it? I must not eat pig, you see."

Making a genuine mistake which I regret to this day, I take "pig" to mean "pork" and I reply dismissively: "Oh no, there's no pig in there. Just egg and banana and some ham. Here, help yourself..."

With evident relish, Mr Shah extracts a sandwich from the top of the pile in the tin and returns to his bench, a few yards away across the picnic area. He sets about devouring his unexpected repast, a smile of satisfied contentment lighting up his face.

As I take up my seat next to him, Selwyn leans towards me and whispers confidentially. "See, you have to be careful, nowadays, Fred. They mustn't eat *any* pig-meat at all. No pork cracklin' for them - or bacon sarnies," There is a long pause. "Or 'am..."

Panic seizes me and I lapse into Shoddy Town speak. "Shit! There wor some 'am sarnies in t'bottom o' mi tin, Selwyn. Ah'd best tell 'im afore 'e gets one darn, in case 'e's gorr an 'am un..."

But it's too late. Mr Shah's hunger-driven mandibles have already fastened round the outer edges of the sandwich which was formerly mine, and he is chewing away ecstatically, a beam of digestive pleasure lighting his face. I race over to him.

"Mr Shah! Mr Shah! Ah"m reight sorry, burr Ah think tha might 'a' tekken an 'am un."

He looks at me, non-plussed. "I apologise, Mr Bootler. I am not understood."

In desperation, and speaking clearly and slowly, I revert to proper teacher-speak: "The sandwich that you are in the process of consuming, Mr Shah, may be of the ham variety."

A glazed look of stricken realisation washes across Mr Shah's face.

His complexion turns ashen and he doubles up, as if paralysed by stomach cramps. He tosses the offending item of food to one side and collapses to the ground in a squatting, supplicant crouch.

With his hands together, he wails plaintively up at the Dales sky: "Oh, please, no," he groans, and proceeds to ram two fingers down his throat as far as they will go. Leaping to his feet, he staggers round the picnic area, bent double and making violent honking noises.

I am taken aback. I had not expected such a deep-seated and violent reaction to a ham sandwich. I follow him, attempting to make placatory noises, but it is to no avail. Mr Shah's anguish is plain for all to see as he lowers himself to his knees, wretching and heaving.

I look back at Selwyn who is in an educational quandary. How can he explain to our party of BHS lads what is amiss with our interpreter? In a forlorn attempt to soothe the now-purple-faced Mr Shah, he picks up my snap-tin and dashes over to us.

" 'Ere, Fred," he gasps as he thrusts the tin towards me.

" Give 'im one of your drinks before he chokes himself to death."

In a panic, I scrabble about in my tin for a drink. To my great relief, I discover not only a small carton of orange-juice but something much more comforting. A rapid assessment of the remaining comestibles reveals that the sarnie which has caused all the bother had *not* included any pig-meat after all. Instead, it had contained a liberal filling of mashed *banana*.

Joyfully, I race over to the kneeling figure. "Mr Shah! Mr Shah! It's alright! You haven't eaten any pig."

But upon extracting his digits from the top end of his oesophagus, Mr Shah is difficult to convince. There is a lull in his honking noises as he speaks: "You tell me I took ham, Mr Bootler. Ham is pig. I must repent and rid myself..."

He re-inserts his fingers and there are yet more violent honking sounds.

"No, Mr Shah. It was a *banana* sarnie -- honest!" I state as soothingly as I can. But Mr Shah is unconsolable. He trembles and groans as he staggers about, clutching his stomach with his free hand.

I look round, desperately seeking help from any quarter. Still keen to display his considerable linguistic prowess, Iftikhar Patel, races to the rescue across the car park.

After my hasty explanation about the constituents of Mr Shah's sandwich, Iftikhar grabs him by the shoulders and begins to jabber furiously in Gujerati. I catch the words "sandwich" and "snap-tin" as Mr Shah's face visibly lightens and the honking noises subside. Iftikhar smiles triumphantly over his shoulder.

"I tell him, sir! No pig - just pineapple. He's OK now."

In a minute or so, Mr Shah is well enough to address me directly: "Thank you so much, Mr Bootler. I am so happy. You are greatly kind to me and I accept with great apology for misunderstanding. But I ask you kindly - do you have just one more pineapple sarnie for me, because I still hunger for one..."

"Of course," I sigh resignedly, passing an internal memo not to enter into any discussion about the differences between "banana" and "pineapple" with particular reference to sandwich-fillings.

I smile benignly as Mr Shah munches away happily, sitting cross-legged at the end of his bench...

So that incident remains etched vividly into the memory-plates of my teaching career. But it wasn't as if every dinner-time was filled with exciting entertainment like that. Far from it!

In my day, dinner time represented a focal point in every scholastic 24 hours and another hour's graft in my weekly educational schedule.

In addition to collecting the dinner-money first thing on Monday mornings, we teachers were also allowed to supervise queues and dining rooms once every seven days, when your "Dinner Duty" came around. We just accepted it as part of the job.

So for thirty years or so, week in, week out, I supervised queues of famished children, drooling expectantly at the dining room doors. I patrolled noisy refectories where they indulged in the most important educational period of their school day. Lessons paled into insignificance compared to this hour's worth of hunger-gratification.

And how well I remember *that* feeling from my own school days in the late 1950's at Batley Grammar School...

The mid-day bell announces the impending arrival of nourishment, I salivate expectantly and prepare to make the dash to the dinner queue on the tiled corridor of the lower floor. A weedy short-trousered twelve year-old, I had to stay at school for my dinner because I lived too far away to take a mid-day bus-trip home. As a result, I came under the close scrutiny of Blackhouse, Dedman and Clogg. They were not a firm of Shoddy Town solicitors, but three Big, Bad Buggers [B.B.B.'s] from 5B.

In those days, you went for your dinner into the dining room adjacent to the magnificent School Library.

There was a centre aisle in the low, wooden-floored room either side of which, tables of eight were laid out ready for an invasion of famished Batley lads. At the far end of the room, the teachers [who preferred the term "masters" and who were also hungry] sat at a long table, well away from the starving hoi-polloi.

We sat at the tables of eight, each "supervised" by an older lad. For some mysterious reason, this method of dishing out dinner-time grub was known as "family service". That was clearly somebody's idea of a joke because it was about as near to a caring, family atmosphere as Birkenshaw is to Ravensthorpe if you're a Shoddy Town thoroughbred.

Now, when it comes to matters of the belly, Big Lads will go out of their way to ensure more than a fair share-out compared to Little Lads - and B.B.B. Blackhouse was no exception. A swarthy, brute of a bully from Healey, he always made sure that his partners in dinner-time table supervision were permanently allocated seats at his right and left hand. So when it was time to divvy up the dinner, it's not too difficult to guess who got significantly more than the lion's share.

I well recall a share-allocation of steak-pie one February day in 1957.

For some reason, I'd arrived in the dining-room queue later than scheduled, so I would not be taking the coming meal in the happy company of any of the lads in my form who were my usual dinner-time chums. On this occasion, I became a "spare" at the end of the line, a "nobbut" to be allocated to any vacant place which might have arisen through the absence of its regular incumbent.

The hand-bell is rung by the master "on duty" and a silence falls over the entire dining-room full of boys. Any talking during the subsequent activity is punishable with the reward of a Saturday morning detention, so the allocation of spare seats takes place in an enforced, unnatural hush.

The master in charge shoves me towards a place at a table occupied by the afore-mentioned trio. They leer visciously at me as I make my desolate way down to a seat at the end of the table, next to the wall. I note their curled lips dripping saliva, and I am convinced that I am about to feature as their main course.

The still silence is broken as the Masters and the Sixth Formers chant the grace reverently and the rest of us say a muffled "Amen". The hand-bell is rung once more to permit talking, and I prepare to be eaten alive. The master in charge licks his lips expectantly, takes his seat at the Staff table and another dinner-time unfolds...

A grey, metal oblong tray appears at the head of the table. B.B.B. Blackhouse wields a WRCC knife and divides up the contents into eight. Apprentice B.B.B. Dedman takes the tip of his WRCC spoon and slides a thumb-nail portion of mashed potato onto the plate.

Co-Apprentice B.B.B. Clogg places a similar portion of emerald green cabbage about six inches away from the other items of nourishment on the plate. With a dark, threatening look, he passes it to me. This is my allocation of today's dinner.

I say nothing as I lift my knife and fork. To utter one syllable in protest at my meagre rations would mean a sound thrashing on the way home. Big Bad Blackhouse lived up Healey, so he caught the same bus as me, and he'd already shown no lack of reticence in coming forward to beat the living daylights out of me, for no reason at all.

Some weeks ago, during the dark days of winter, he'd fancied some home-time entertainment aboard our Number 21 Yorkshire Woollen District Transport Company Omnibus. He'd waited until we were rounding the corner of Mayman Lane and then he'd leapt out of his seat to get me.

"Oh, thee!" he'd growled. "What tha lookin' at?"

In my naive innocence, I was about to tell him that I was just gazing at the awesome Shoddy Town splendour of Taylor's Blakeridge Mill out of the bus-window, but he struck before I could say a word.

Fastening his big, swarthy mauler round my neck, he'd smacked my head against the cold steel of the rear passenger-seat hand-rail on the upper deck...

And now, I sit in my little seat at the end of the dinner table, recalling the resulting three days of throbbing headache as the pudding course arrives. It brings with it an interesting variation in the Family Service method of victual allocation.

This time, I receive no golden sponge pudding at all but, in a beneficent gesture, I am allowed a little custard.

B.B.B. Dedman has been awarded the responsibility of custard apportionment, so he dips his fork into the grey steel jug and lifts off the rubbery, yellow putrescence of the skin. It is deposited on my pudding plate and forwarded to me for consumption. I manfully force it down my gullet with a drink of tepid WRCC water, not daring to utter a word...

This awful experience of a long-gone dinner-time remains with me as I make my way through my teaching life. ...

And right now, I stand in the cold, draughty dining-room of 1970's Earlsheaton School, all prepared to supervise the coming mid-day break. I recall the helplessness in that threatening situation of my own schooldays as I watch the files of young, salivating children passing by on their way towards their dinner-time tucker.

Keeping a watchful eye on proceedings, I trust that, during the intervening dozen or so years, we've moved on to a much fairer system of victual allocation.

But what have we here, before my very eyes? Tables of eight, all set out for family service; boys in one half of the dining-room and girls in the other. At the head of each table, steel grey trays of delightfully tasty pies, prepared lovingly that very morning by Mrs Hartley and her team of white-smocked cooks, in the rattle and clatter of our school kitchens.

And at the head of one particular table, hunched menacingly over the steel-grey tray, sits a huge square-jawed Fifth Year kid called Tomlinson. He is in charge of the table's affairs and carries the heavy responsibility for victual allocation. *Another* Big Bad Bugger from 5B...

With vivid recollections of 1957 and the skin of the custard, I nonchalantly patrol the dining-room to maintain order.

Craftily, I pretend not to notice the huge mountain of delicious dinner-time fare piled high on Tomlinson's plate or the scrappy morsel on that of the tiny, emaciated First Year lad at the end of the table. I wait in the wings, over by the large windows, ready to pounce.

Just as B.B.B. Tomlinson has raised his knife and fork, I strike. With an admirable sense of dramatic timing, I leap over to descend like an avenging angel.

"I'll have that, lad," I announce judicially to all who might be listening, and whip away Tomlinson's amply charged plate. I walk purposefully to the far end of the table.

B.B.B.'s jaw drops to trouser-belt level as I slide the dinner-mountain in front of the wide-eyed First Year and deftly whip away his morsel.

Returning to the top of the table, and with a suitably theatrical gesture, I present the Big Bad Bugger with the Measly Minute Morsel.

" 'Ere, lad," I whisper, employing Shoddy Town Speak to emphasise my moral point. "This scoddy little bit is thine. An' dooan't let me catch thi cheatin' ivver aggean."

First Year Lad cannot believe his luck. He smacks his thin, narrow lips in anticipatory digestive delight and sets about the food-mountain like a starving vacuum-cleaner.

B.B.B. Tomlinson munches unenthusiastically, mumbles downwards at his plate and moans unintelligibly about value for money.

I fancy I hear the words "An' Ahs'll tell mi father," but I remain unimpressed.

A grim smile of satisfaction lights my face as I stand over them both, arms folded, to supervise complete and effective consumption of said victuals.

In the dining-room chatter about me, I hear an echo from 1957 and see again the rubbery, yellow putrescence of custard-skin as it flops lifelessly onto my plate. The taste of tepid WRCC water re-surfaces at the back of my throat, and the cold steel of the rear passenger-seat hand-rail on the Number 21 bus clouts me once more on the back of my head.

But by now, the ghosts of Blackhouse, Dedman and Clogg have been well and truly laid, and another satisfactory dinner-time draws to a close...

***

THE MAN  IN BLACK

It's a fine September morning in 1987 on Wellhouse fields. The air is clear, the sky is blue and the view over Crossley Fields to Norristhorpe, Dewsbury Moor and all points North is drenched in golden, autumn sunshine.

Sixteen or so football-booted youngsters between the ages of nine and fourteen run hither and thither on the school football field, leaping and diving, wrestling and rolling, whistling and shouting.

The shadow of the goalpost falls across their discarded clothes, an assortment of discarded bikes and a net-bag full of footballs. It comes to rest at the booted feet of an ageing, balding, six-foot bloke in a blue "Adidas" track-suit - the Coach.

Coach delivers several blasts of his Acme Thunderer whistle and announces, as he has done on football pitches throughout the Heavy Woollen District of the past thirty years: "Right, lads! Gather round!"

Over a period five minutes, the general cavorting, shouting and jumping gradually subsides, and the group sits on the floor around their Coach...

"Now remember, boys. When you go out onto the field, there's two things that should be buzzing round in your heads..."

I looked down at the sixteen or so upturned faces, eyes fixed on me, as if I was some footballing icon. Thirty two pairs of peepers all focussed on *me* as I deliver the footballing maxims which have stood me in good stead for the past forty-five Shoddy Town years. Waves of sporting emotion and pride well up in my breast. I feel like "one of the lads" all over again and I drift off on a train of football-orientated thought.

I'm having the time of my life, talking, living and breathing football with a bunch of youngsters who all share my enthusiasm for the Beautiful Game. Every time they take the field, memories of long-gone encounters re-surface, and I am proud to be their Coach.

These lads turn out every Saturday morning in the Mirfield and District Church League and we adults accompany them on their sporting travels.

This Church League is the only one of its kind in the country, since it allows boys of nine up to the age of fourteen to play in the same team. League Rules state that combined ages of a team must not total more than 133, so if the Manager/Coach is any good at Maths, he can, if he wants to win every game played, field a side with a great number of 14 year-olds. This means, however, that he must balance the side with an obligatory smattering of nine year-olds.

As a manager, if you take up this last named option, you're probably assured of League and Cup success. Those nine year olds who are only in your side to make up the numbers and to comply with League rules will spend their Saturday mornings frozen stiff, draped in a shirt which is six sizes too big for them. They will run about on the wing like headless chickens always a safe and secure twenty yards away from the nasty, hurtful ball.

But *we* are Wellhouse Moravians FC, and the man in charge of *our* team affairs, Our Revered Leader, would never, in a month of Sabbaths, stoop to such sharp practices. ORL is the ebullient, charismatic Reverend Robert Hopcroft who does all the mugging about required in the running of a team of youngsters like ours.

Diminutive, moustachioed Bob is our inspiration - a live-wire of Christian goodness and our vicar at the Moravian Church. Amongst the population of our district, he commands enormous respect, but in addition to all that, he is mad about football.

Bob's avid enthusiasm for the Beautiful Game keeps us all going throughout the dark, cold winter mornings. We thrive on the discipline and sense of fair play which he offers as a character-building education in the Finer Things in Life, including Football.

However, Bob's presence as Team Manager on a Saturday morning is a severely limiting factor in our touch-line language. Expressions which were commonplace in my Yorkshire Old Boys League playing days such as: "Get stuffed, Ref!" or "If that wor off-side, Ah'll show my bare arse on t' Town 'All steps!" now have to be tempered to take due regard of the dog-collar in our midst.

Sadly, such expressions lose a little in transposition:

"I say, Referee, why not pay a visit to Abdul the Taxidermist" or "In the event of that being a correct decision regarding off-side, Referee, I will gladly expose my nether regions on Long Causeway".

In addition, Bob insists on "playing the game." This means that *every* player gets a fair slice of the footballing cake and every lad who signs on for Wellhouse Moravians FC gets a chance to play in the team on a Saturday morning, regardless of ability. This often annoyed the Coach...

A bored snort from the back of the assembled group of seated lads shakes me out of my philosophical rêverie and I resume my coaching session:

"First thing buzzing in your brain: *The referee is always right, even when he's wrong,*" I state, categorically and unequivocally.

With this basic sporting tenet, several of the Littl'uns in the Wellhouse Moravians football squad are confused.

"'Ow can 'e be reight when 'e's wrong," they puzzle. The older lads sigh in exasperated fashion and look skywards because they are seasoned campaigners and they've heard it all before. They know what's coming next.

"Without a referee," I lecture, "we haven't a game. There'd be nobody to make important decisions, so the game would stop. The referee is the most important bloke on the field. What he says goes," I continue, switched now to teacher-mode, and in full flow. "His decision is final, so we just accept it and get on with the game."

A sudden lapse into Shoddy Town speak produces my final, conclusive teaching point: " 'E weeant change 'is mind, will 'e? So no chelpin', gripin' or belly-achin'. Just gerrout theer an' laik..."

The eyes of several of the younger ones, at whom this teaching point is aimed, have glazed over. One or two of the others are being distracted by the procreative activity of two mongrels at the top end of the field, near the green iron fence. They are going at it like star-cross'd lovers.

I need to regain the squad's attention and bring them back to the world of Association Football. With volume control switched to maximum, and returning to teacher-speak, I brandish my Acme Thunderer whistle with a dramatic flourish. I boom out my next question at top whack: "What have I got in my hand?"

Some of the inattentive Littl'uns jump with fright and one of them cowers down behind his bike.

"Yes, it's my whistle and it controls the game, doesn't it?" I continue. "Now - what's that second thing which should be buzzing round your brain during a game?"

Restraining himself from making any observation about me having my hand on my whistle in public, 14 year-old Broughie provides the answer to my coaching question with a resigned sigh: "Knock it wide, Fred," and the group breaks away for a kick-about ...

Our practice game proceeds and coaching points emerge at regular intervals. I stop play with a blast of the whistle, demonstrate a vital coaching point to any of the lads who have lost interest in the two mongrels, and re-start the game.

I'm in total charge. At the sound of my whistle, everybody stops and looks expectantly towards me. When the whistle blows, the Referee is always right.

My mind has switched to automatic pilot and I begin to drift away to the touchlines of yester-year...

In my yellow 'keeper's jersey, I join the other lads in their dark-blue/light-blue quartered shirts as we trek along the cinder track at the top of the school. We turn left up the pavement onto Carlinghow Hill to make our way up the steep slope to our school football field, some three hundred yards away. This will be the setting for our 1962-63 Season, Batley Grammar School First XI endeavour for the next hour and a half.

It is not going to be easy. We sum up our chances on the way up to the field. Firstly, our opposition today is Normanton Grammar School who always give us a very competitive game. In Shoddy Town speak: "They're bahna gie us a reight towellin' ".

Secondly, flakes of snow lace the bitterly cold wind as we pass through the gate at the bottom of the field. The sky darkens and the wind begins to whip ice-spicules at our bared flesh.

And thirdly, our designated Man-in-Black is Mr Gill, [English teacher] who knows sod all about the Beautiful Game. But at least we have a referee, a public-spirited, unselfish teacher who is willing to forego a Saturday morning in bed to witness our tactical meanderings around the *Billiard Table*.

That was the euphemistic name of our BGS pitch at the top of Carlinghow Hill. Named long ago by some joker with a severe geometrical deficiency, that yester-year field of dreams was anything but the flat green baize of snooker halls.

Entry to the field was gained via a five-barred gate and the bottom goals stood hard by a hawthorn hedge at the road-side. The lower half of the pitch had only a gentle slope towards the half-way line, which was not unusual at local Shoddy Town venues in the far-off 1960's. But by the time adventurous forwards had dribbled their arduous ways towards their opponents' goal at the top end, they were faced with an ascent of North-Face-of-the-Eiger proportions if they wanted to gain entry to the penalty area.

Crampons and a variety of climbing ropes were required to cross the white line at the edge, along with breathing apparatus in order to cope with the rarified atmosphere. Once in the attacking zone, however, visiting forwards would find a relatively flat penalty area in which to swiftly change back into football boots before firing in a shot on goal.

The site of that First XI pitch of long ago is now a tasteful, bungalowed development of domiciles, all warm and welcoming in their suburban Shoddy Town splendour. But little do the residents know that they live in the precise location where many of us have shed very high-quality blood in the BGS cause.

The five-barred gate at the bottom of the field has given way to a tar-mac entrance with the tasteful logo "Hollybank Avenue" as its modern name. To us Batley lads of yore, however, it will always be the Billiard Table...

Today, we climb the gate to do battle once more.

Following our traditionally sporting BGS code of conduct, we sieze the bottom goals for our pre-match warm up. Such selfless action allows the Normanton lads the dizzy heights of the top penalty area for their pre-match kick-in. It is our secret and fervent hope that some of them might die of oxygen starvation before the kick-off at 10.00am.

We await the arrival of our referee in the biting, north-east wind with its flurries of snow, testing our survival techniques to the full. Foregoing the pleasures of a spot of pre-match kicking-in, we prance up and down, hands buried deep in shorts, and attempt to stave off the groping talons of frost-bite and/or exposure.

Ten minutes pass before I hear Referee Gill's educated tones. Leaning over the five-barred gate, he shouts above the howling wind: "Ah, Butler, would you and one or two of the others open the gate for me..."

Puzzled looks are exchanged between members of the First XI.

Sporting a chequered deer-stalker hat, Referee Gill is dressed in a large tweed overcoat and yellow muffler. Bemused as to the whereabouts of his refereeing gear, we open the gate, as instructed, and Gill's shape disappears into the increasing snow flurries down Carlinghow Hill.

"What we doin' this for," groans Skipper Jack Hirst as we heave and strain at the gate. "What's 'e want t'gate open for?"

Skipper's queries are soon answered.

From a little way down the hill towards school, we hear the furious revving of a car engine. Moments later, a green Morris Minor roars in through the gate and threads its way erratically up the left-hand touchline.

After a series of complicated manouevres and several three-point turns, it pulls up, facing the Billiard Table pitch, spot on the half-way line.

Now because we're all at the Grammar school and thus know absolutely everything there is to know about absolutely everything, we soon twig what Referee Gill is up to.

From his position on the half-way line, our week-day English teacher is about to conduct his Saturday morning refereeing duties all snug and warm in the interior of his Morris Minor - with the engine running and the heater on "*maximum*"! We players, having bared our flesh to the ever-increasing, icy east wind, were expected to get on with the game.

By now, some of the Normanton lads who have not suffered the effects of oxygen-starvation in the top penalty area, wander down from the heights. In their South Yorkshire twang, they begin to ask leading questions. "Wass gewin' on 'ere, then? Wheer's t'ref? When we kickin' off, like?

Embarrassed beyond belief, we BGS lads explain lamely how the coming ninety minutes is likely to pan out, with particular reference to refereeing arrangements. To their credit, the Normanton lads accept with good grace. They are going to give us a towelling anyway, and they are keen to play football. Moreover, just like us, they are desperate to generate some blood-flow to their freezing extremities which are in imminent danger of dropping off.

They place the ball on a snow-covered centre-spot and rub their hands expectantly.

The kick-off is prompted by a muffled peep from deep within the upholstered warmth of the Morris Minor on the touchline, and at last our game is under way.

Throughout the subsequent period of play, whilst concentrating on playing football, we all have the added responsibility of straining an ear for the distant sound of the referee's whistle in the event of any dispute. It is a noticeable feature of the whole game that many players on the far side of the pitch played the entire ninety minutes with one hand cupped round an attentive ear...

The snow flurries increase, rendering visibility difficult, but, nevertheless, our match proceeds. Over on the far side, wily, scheming Normanton inside forward is up-ended.

There is a muffled whistle from afar, and Gill leans out of the car window. "I say, Blamires! That was a bit of a fierce tackle. Normanton free kick, just there," he booms at us, and points a vague finger.

Our Saturday morning fun unfolds.

With the exception of one or two murmurings regarding the validity of Referee Gill's off-side decisions - " 'Ow the 'ell can 'e see fro' over theer, the daft bugger," - we manage to complete a shortened game as the snow descends. The result is a 0-0 draw, and first back into the warmth of the changing-rooms is the very mobile Referee Gill...

What strikes me from this end of the telescope of time is that we did not question that bizarre technique of Sport for All. This was 1963. Teacher's word was law. And at least, we had a referee...

The immense value of the referee and all that he stood for was really brought home to me as my latter-day footballing career began to move towards its twilight years, long after the days of Mr Gill's Morris Minor.

By the early 1970's, I'd become accustomed to playing in games where there was an officially appointed referee.

Highly trained and excellently qualified, such people would arrive for a game and change into a bona fide referee's uniform. These Men-in-Black carried an aura of officialdom about their persons and thus commanded our sincere respect.

It was my privilege to meet many such chaps as the seasons came and went. I even become friendly with one or two of them over the years, since they often officiated at several games in which I played.

The crowning glory of my largely forgettable footballing career came in 1976 when it was an immense honour to be elected skipper of the Wheelwright Old Boys Third XI at the age of 31.

I proudly led our ageing team of footballing has-beens onto the football fields of the West Riding every Saturday afternoon, prepared to do battle in the West Yorkshire Old Boys' League, Division Three. But I'd failed to realise that such a lofty position in the hierarchy of the club carried with it a set of ancillary duties for which I had *not* bargained...

No longer was it a matter of turning up on a Saturday afternoon for ninety minutes of frolicking fun. Now, prior to every match, heavy responsibilities weighed down on my Skipper's shoulders.

It was the Captain's job, I discovered, to select the side and to find last-minute replacements when someone's wife issued an ultimatum. It also fell to the Skipper to detail team-members [and assist them] to put up goal-nets in the freezing cold, thirty minutes before the game.

After the ninety minutes' worth of frolicking fun, Skipper's responsibilities weren't over.

He had to go round with the hat to collect match fees in order pay the referee. And as if that wasn't enough, with frozen fingers still numb from the previous sporting toil in winter's icy grasp, the Captain had to complete a Match Report Card, to be signed by the Man-in-Black, and remember to post it off to the League Results Secretary on Monday morning.

It soon became apparent to me that none of these tasks was remotely connected to the joyful activity of kicking a ball about on a football pitch. Rather, they were allocated to any mug who was daft enough to accept the responsibility of Captaincy. But amongst all those responsibilities, the one I came to detest the most was when the referee blobbed/ducked/went AWOL/got lost in Dewsbury - in plain English, failed to turn up.

Our Old Boys League was quite clear in its written instructions on what to do in such circumstances, as I discovered the first time it happened when I was in charge.

Desperately thumbing through the Official Handbook at 2.58pm one Saturday afternoon, I found the following entry:

> Rule 6[b]   *In the event of the referee appointed to*
> *a match failing to fulfil his appointment....*
> *the home club will be held responsible for*
> *providing a referee*

Oh joy! Here we are at kick-off time, and I must now find a referee!

And at this point, I discover another of the Captain's responsibilities.

The home side would have to face the coming encounter with only ten men whilst one of their number undertook refereeing duties for the afternoon. Skipper would nominate the ref. for the day.

The notion of refereeing a game when one has turned up to play in it was not received with overjoyed enthusiasm amongst the members of the Wheelwright Old Boys Third XI.

Eyes would be averted, bootlaces would suddenly require urgent attention, toilet cubicles would fill to over-flowing and items of kit would be inadvertently left in the car. Team members took desperate measures to avoid my ultimate approach. So there was nothing else for it...

Sighing wistfully, donning my track-suit and grasping my standard 1966, WRCC issue, Acme Thunderer in my right hand, I take to the field to act as a stand-in Man-in-Black.

Well, at least we have a referee. "But I'm buggered if I'm doin' it next week," I mutter to myself as I lock up the changing-rooms before taking the field, Match Day Security Arrangements being yet another of the Captain's responsibilities.

As the seasons roll by and we prepare each Saturday for the coming home encounter, Yours Truly is *always*, without exception, utterly overjoyed when the Man in Black announces his arrival in the changing room. As he walks to a quiet, unoccupied spot to begin changing into his official uniform, I have to restrain myself both physically and emotionally, from rushing over to him and embracing him like a long-lost brother.

So it was my fortnightly pleasure to welcome a succession of Men in Black between my twilight years of 1975 and 1979...

It's 2.40pm on a cold, dismal Saturday in January. Up at

Earlsheaton School [our home venue in those days], I clamber into my specially re-inforced whale-bone jock-strap to prepare for the coming ninety minutes' worth of fun. I keep one anxious eye on the changing-room door, for our appointed official has yet to turn up.

By 2.50pm, I begin to rummage the depths of my bag for my Acme Thunder as a wave of disappointment washes over me.

Dismally, I pull on my track-suit and miserably prepare for yet another ninety minute session as a stand-in Man-in-Black.

I trudge dejectedly outside into the bitter January wind. It's beginning to rain and all I've got to look forward to is ninety minutes [plus extra-time] of running around and blowing a whistle.

But fear not! Round the corner at the top of the school, waving apologetically and ringing his cycle bell, our appointed official hoves into sight - Mr Auty, The Whistling Postman.

Tall and angular, with serious, dark, expressionless eyes, a gaunt look and a Prussian haircut, Mr Auty dismounts from his GPO standard issue red bicycle outside the changing-rooms. He bends down to unfasten his cycle clips, straightens up to his full height and reaches into the inside pocket of his large, dark-blue GPO overcoat.

Extracting his West Riding Old Boys' League Match Appointment Card, he scrutinizes it carefully. "Wheelwright Thirds?" he enquires " 'Ave Ah got t'reight place?"

Resisting a sudden show of relieved emotion, I hold off from giving him a great big hug.

"That's us," I greet him enthusiastically, hands firmly clasped behind my back. "Good to see yer, ref!"

Raising the substantial shoulder-pads of his overcoat, Mr Auty addresses me officially now as he makes his way into the changing rooms.

"Sorry Ah'm a bit late, Captain," he says. "Ah got caught up in a special delivery job to Ossett, burr Ah'm 'ere nar, so we'd best gerron wi' it. By, burrit's a bit parky, innit?" And he rubs his boney hands together as he makes his way to an unoccupied corner.

Already, I've ripped off my track-suit and tossed aside my Acme Thunderer. Today, I shall be playing centre-half and not acting as a Man-in-Black stand-in. Today, at least, we have a *proper* referee.

Twenty minutes into the game, during which the wind has increased, the temperature has dropped several degrees and the rain has started to lash horizontally, there is a piercing blast from Mr Auty's whistle. All players grind to an astounded halt.

"What's that for, ref?"

"Nowt," is the Postman's reply. "Just gather round 'ere a minute."

He calls the members of both sides to a point in the centre circle. We gather round, leaning into the howling gale with its stabbing blasts of icy rain, hands down shorts for warmth.

"What's up, ref?"

The Whistling Postman's teeth are chattering as he delivers his stunning ultimatum. "Iiit's ter   cccowd fer me," he stammers. "Ah think Ah must bi cccatchin' t'flu or sssummat. Yer'll aveter cccarry on thisens. Ah'm off ooam ter bbbed..."

And he leaves the scene.

Ten minutes later, we see him cycle off, head bowed against the driving rain, round the corner of the school building, never to be seen again.

Well, we *had* a ref. but now he's gone. Dejectedly downcast, Yours Truly pulls on a track suit and reaches for the Acme Thunderer...

The only game I've played in, and *almost* wished that we *hadn't* had a Man-in-Black to officiate, occurred off Dewsbury Road in Leeds, next to some allotments, midway between the Broadway Hotel and the Crescent Bingo Hall.

It was a fine Saturday afternoon towards the end of the 1978 season. The relegation and promotion issues in our Third Division had long since ceased to concern either Wheelwright Thirds or Old Cockburnians Fourths, our opposition for the day. We were looking forward to a gentle frolick in the sunshine on the drying surface of a big flat pitch.

Our referee for the day, a diminutive, balding chap in his fifties with horn-rimmed glasses, had turned up well before the appointed hour. He took to a small corner of the changing-rooms and began to don his official uniform.

I remember thinking to myself that he must be a *very good* referee because he wore two watches - one on either wrist below the crisply ironed white cuffs of his black official's shirt. And, in addition to the ones he placed carefully in his top pocket, he tucked a spare pencil and notebook down his sock. This was obviously not a

"Ah think Ah must bi cccatchin' t'flu or sssummat."

referee with whom to trifle. We would have to be on our best Wheelwright Old Boys behaviour.

My abiding memory of this particular Man-in-Black, however, concerned his seeing apparatus. The hornrimmed lenses of his spectacles were the bottle-bottomed type, with an estimated magnification factor of about fifty. But when he removed them to leave the changing-room, I recall that he had the look of Lenny the Cross-eyed Lion. And he was going to take to the field *without* his glasses.

We looked at each other grimly. A sense of foreboding washed over us all as we went out to do battle. It was only a couple of matches ago when we'd taken the field to play Old Centralians and our referee for the day had displayed similarly odd characteristics.

That Man-in-Black had taken the field apologetically after a climb over the perimeter fence at the West Park ground. But that wasn't the only wayward factor. The greatest problem for all players in that particular game was that our referee was unable to communicate readily in our mother tongue. Mr Taj Mohammed had but a smattering of English, and as smatterings go, it was, in truth, only the slightest smear.

Apart from "Yes", "No", and "Off-side", his apparent knowledge of the technical jargon of football was nil. We marvelled at the fact that he'd passed his Referees' Badge as all ensuing decisions during the current match were communicated in sign language.

Trying to ascertain his frequent awards of free-kicks proved to be an extremely difficult task.

We spent much of the game in a great deal of frantic toing and froing as he waved his arms about like a wild dervish on Guinness. And he uttered not one explanatory word as to the reasons for his often puzzling decisions.

The blast of his whistle pierces the afternoon air and we are absolutely certain that he's awarded us a free-kick. We all dash forward, expectantly eager, in a frenzy of attacking activity. You can imagine our dismay as Ref. stands over the ball and points emphatically towards our goal, signifying a free-kick to our opposition.

We turn tail immediately in a frantic rear-guard action. Considerable mental and physical agility is required to make the switch from attacking mode into the defensive one as we charge desperately back towards our goal. In the meantime, Centralians score.

The result of all this hyper-activity was that many of our players were severely knackered by the time Man-in-Black blew for half-time. We resolved to resign *en-bloc*, as a matter of safety first, before the start of the second half. But we couldn't abide the thought of missing a whole half of frolicking fun.

However, that was two Saturdays ago. Today was going to be altogether different...

Today, we take the field in eager anticipation of a good end-of-season game, efficiently supervised by our immaculately turned-out, officially-appointed Man-in-Black. Misgivings about his wayward line of sight as a result of his severely crossed eyes are shelved in the deep recesses of our minds.

We relish the prospect of the impending ninety minutes.

Now, as it happened, I had played several times against today's opposition and, as is a feature of Old Boys football at this level, many players from opposing teams are well known to one another, having played against each other for several seasons.

I well remember a chap from Old Hansonians Seconds who gave me a pet nick-name and who always greeted my entrance into their changing-rooms with the same words of welcome, season after season: "Eh up' lads Here comes Arkle* ageean..."

On this occasion, our game was well under way when the Old Cockburnians centre-forward indulged in a spot of gamesmanship. He was a fair-haired youth of about twenty or so tender years whose name was Grahame, and in all our aerial encounters thus far into the game, Yours Truly had come off best. But on this occasion, as I rose majestically to head away a ball which was plummetting from the heavens and threatening our defence, I hear a gentle call from somewhere behind me: "Leave it, Fred! My ball!"

Believing this to be a tactical message from Brian Hirst, the Rock at the heart of our Wheelwright Defence, I duly duck.

Expecting Brian's hefty booted clearance behind me, I am disappointed. No such clearance is forthcoming because Brian is out on the touchline somewhere, making vital adjustments to his card-board shin-guards.

The friendly instruction to "*Leave it, Fred,* " had been issued by Grahame the Cheat who was able to scoot away from me and slot the ball past Steve Pollitt in our goal.

At the use of such tactics, I am somewhat annoyed.

* Arkle   a famous steeplechaser of the four-legged equine variety

Chasing the Cockburnian goal-scorer as he runs, arms aloft towards the players of his own side, I shout at him: "You cheatin' bugger!" And I shake an angry fist.

Clearly, such an aggressive action is not to our referee's liking. With his little legs whirring like bees' wings at the height of summer, he chases after me.

Meanwhile, I continue my particular pursuit of the cheating bugger. Grahame pursued by me, pursued by the Man-in-Black.

"You wazzock!" I fume. "Is that the only way you can score - by cheatin'?"

"Oi," I hear a call from somewhere behind me. "Oi! Come 'ere!"

The said instruction is addressed to nobody in particular, but I look over my shoulder and notice the Ref. pointing and looking at a spot about 10 nautical degrees west of my current position. So he's not talking to me, is he?

Lapsing into Shoddy Town speak, I continue to harangue Grahame the Cheat.

"Tha couldn't score a reight goal if thi life depended on it, yer cheatin' pillock!"

Again, "Oi, you! Come 'ere!" So this time, I call a temporary halt to my angry outburst and turn round.

Although Ref. is still not pointing directly at me, he is heading in my general direction. When we come within eye-contact range of each other, it is perfectly obvious to me that he is looking at some other player who is probably ten yards or so to my left.

I look over my shoulder to ascertain if it's one our

Wheelwright stalwarts who is in trouble, but there is nobody in that direction, so I shrug my shoulders and walk away.

Having lost contact with Grahame the Cockburnian Cheat who is now being mobbed in congratulatory fashion by his team-mates, I amble over to discuss the general situation with our left back, Alan Austerfield.

"Did you 'ear that pillock call fer that ball, then, Alan," I ask plaintively.

"Well, to be truthful, Fred, I didn't hear a thing," replies Alan, a fellow teacher. "I was having a spot of bother with the elastic in my JS, so I wasn't paying *that* much attention. Look, it seems to be chaffing me across my left buttock..."

"Oi! Thee! Lanky bugger! COME 'ERE!"

At this point, I have a slight inkling that the Man-in-Black is after *me*. Abandoning my close scrutiny of Austerfield's rump, I turn and look.

Sure enough, far below me, pointing an accusing finger straight upwards in the general direction of my midriff, is the Man-in-Black. It is indeed Yours Truly with whom he would like to confer.

I almost came out with my genuinely truthful excuse: "Ref, I *do* apologise. I had no idea that you wanted to address me because you are so cross-eyed, I thought you were looking at somebody ten yards over my shoulder..."

But, besides being an insult, such a genuine explanation of my plight would probably have got me sent off, so I stand, looking humbly down at his diminutive frame.

He launches into a rollicking of mighty, Man-in-Black

proportions, wagging his finger as high up as he could reach, which was somewhere around my breast-bone.

I am accused of ungentlemanly conduct, violent behaviour *and* bringing the game into disrepute. I fully expect an additional indictment for murder, as enraged Man-in-Black fumbles in his pocket for his note-book. His search is fruitless, however, and I am tempted to assist by reminding him that he has a spare down his sock, but that would probably have led to further disciplinary procedures against me.

As it was, and in the absence of his notebook, Ref gave me a severe rollicking which was shot venomously at a point some ten feet wide of my left shoulder.

But at least we had a referee...

Some thirty years after that end-of-season incident, I am on the touchline of yet another concluding game. This time, it's the 1986-87 season, and it's an encounter with Mackenzie Methodists, the leading side in the Church League.

Lacking half-a-dozen or so fourteen year old lads [with beards] for selection purposes, our Wellhouse Moravians Management Team, led by the Reverend Bob and assisted by Coach Yours Truly and Assistant Coach Ken Jowett, has taken this end-of-season opportunity to give some of our younger players the experience of a full-blooded League game.

We are being hammered out of sight.

Our referee for the game is a sincere, well-meaning church member from the front benches of our opposition's congregation. He is anxious to see young lads enjoying a game of football, but this encounter barely falls into such a category. Wave after wave of Mackenzie Big Lads [with beards] bear down on our goals, and score after score is notched up.

Their twenty-third goal is quite definitely off-side.

"Oi, Ref," I shout, purple-faced with rage at the injustice of it all.

With due consideration for the fact that I am standing within five yards of a Man of the Cloth, I remonstrate from the touchline with the Man-in-Black in suitably moderated language:

"Aren't we playing to the Queensbury Rules, then, Ref? He was a mile off-side when he got that pass..."

The Reverend Hopcroft sidles over to me and enters Missionary Mode as he calms me down:

"Now then, Fred! Remember: *The referee is always right, even when he's wrong...*"

***

AND  **FINALLY**

My mother used to have a little plaque which stood on our mantle-piece for as long as I can remember. If you looked at it closely, you'd see, in one corner, a picture of an idyllic little cottage at the side of a winding woodland track. The sun was shining on the roses round the door frame and the door of the cottage was slightly ajar, tempting you to tarry a while.

The track wound its way into the wooded distance and led your eye to a gilt-edged scroll with some ornate lettering on it. The words said: "*I shall pass this way but once...*"

As a lad, I often wondered at the wistful wisdom of those words. What *could* they mean? What was the unknown event which occurred '*but once...*'?

Looking back now, I can understand that wise saying which just about sums up my life, ever since my Mum and Dad brought me to the Heavy Woollen District in 1958.Luckily, I've been allowed just the one go at living and growing up in the Dewsbury and Batley of dark, satanic mills fame, even though I'm not a native of 'God's Own County'. So now, I've become a part of my surroundings and there's nowhere else I want to be.

I've passed this way but once, and it's been a fun-filled pleasure-trip. I've sauntered up the snickets of boyhood mischief, frolicked down the ginnels of laughter and fun, *and* I've been privileged to grow up alongside genuine Shoddy Town folk.

Of course, many of the people and places which figured large in my adolescent memory are long-since departed, but they're far from forgotten. They linger about in the fond recollections of my spotty youth...

Broadbent's little green shop at the bottom of Carlinghow Hill, where we used to buy penny drinks on a hot summer's afternoon following our BGS academic toils, has long since been pulled down. But in quiet moments, I still nip in there, feeling flush. Along with my penny drink in its green plastic cup, I buy a penny bag of 'kay-li'. I can still taste its gritty sweetness on the end of my saliva-soaked index finger as I walk out onto the pavement...

And sometimes, standing there in my adolescent dreams, if I shut my eyes and try really hard, I can hear the rhythmic tramp of marching KOYLI feet. The Batley Grammar School Founder's Day Parade makes its way down the hill behind me and out onto Bradford Road.

In the afternoon sunshine, we wheel left down the middle of the main road, a column of lads and masters, three deep. Traffic negotiates its busy way round us as we march solemnly to the Parish Church where we celebrate the origins of BGS.

But I'm not all that concerned about William Lee and 1612AD. I'm far more interested in 1959, 'Lipstick on your Collar' by Connie Francis, 'Charlie Brown' by The Coasters and in getting to the end of the Church Service.

As son as this BGS ritual is over, I'll be racing up Branch Road and along Commercial Street to Dorothy's Coffee Bar, opposite the Wilton Arms. Some of the lasses from the Girls' Grammar School might be in there, and there's one raven-haired beauty who's hinted that she might appreciate my company on some future occasion. I begin to warm to the idea.

If I get lucky, I'll arrange to meet her outside the BonBon Cafe at the far end of Dewsbury Bus Station this coming Saturday night. And if my luck is *really* in, she might agree to accompany me to the Pioneers picture house. After our trip up the lift to the cinema on the top floor, I shall tremble with youthful delight at the prospect of *double* seats for all that kissing and cuddling...

Seconds later, my adolescent bubble has burst asunder in devastating disappointment. The Coffee Bar is empty and outside on the pavement, I am miserable - stood up, forlorn and at a lose end.

I consult my Ingersoll wrist-watch with its brown leather strap. There's at least half an hour before the next Number 20 bus [Leeds-Mirfield via Batley] is due to arrive in the Bus Station and I pause to reflect on my subsequent course of action. I could turn right and nip down Hick Lane to 'Charlie's Pie and Pea 'Oil' for a bite to eat.

"Burrit's nobbut 'alf-past three," I whisper to myself, "an' 'e weeant be open yet..."

Or I could stroll along Bradford Road to Mad Jack's at the bottom of Field Hill. I've only a tanner in my pocket, so that will just about cover the threepenny bus-fare home *and* leave enough for the smoker's bargain on offer at the said emprium - one Woodbine and a match -'for your smoking pleasure'.

Seconds later, in my mind's eye, there I am, leaning up against the wall at the bottom of Branch Road. If I hang around here for long enough, I might meet that lass I'm trying to get keen about when the Girls' Grammar School closes for the day.

I light up, quietly humming to myself.

The strains of 'Come Softly to Me' by The Fleetwoods and 'Dream Lover' by Bobby Darin float back through the air-waves of time. I settle down to await the Grammar School lasses coming down the hill opposite. The deep pull on my forty-two year old Woodbine yields a taste as sweet and satisfying as the nectar of the Gods.

It's twenty past now, and the big red Number 20 bus will be pulling up alongside the Bus Station at the top of Branch Road. A chance meeting with the girl of my dreams on her way home from school has disappeared forever. So I'm out of luck.

Under a dark cloud of adolescent disappointment, I sprint off towards the Bus Station. It's time to catch the last nostalgic bus home from the Shoddy Towns of yester-year and to grow up...

The Dewsbury and Batley of my spotty youth have long since changed into modern townships, befitting the 21st Century. But if I try very hard indeed, those townscapes of yester-year loom serenely above the mists of time. Newsome's Mill chimney still belches thick, black smoke, the side-streets are once again cobbled over and there's always a special chapter on 'The Shoddy Towns' in Geography text-books the world over.

I've had a wonderful time to say I'm not a native. After forty-six years, I'm still living the life, walking the walk and talking the talk of a regular shoddy Town Lad. I've even been allowed to steal a nostalgic look down the ginnel of time gone by and to peep up the snicket of misty memories.

And now it's time to call it a day and to bring down the curtain. Unless - like so many of my generation - I've still got time enough left to nip down that ginnel for just one more 'sly swaller'.

After all, I shall pass this way but once...

$$***$$

SHODDY TOWN SPEAK

Throughout Batley and Dewsbury, our everyday mode of speech is a never-ending delight to the ear of the resident non-native. However, to those from foreign climes, it may sound like a garbled collection of gutteral rumblings. Imagine, then, *my* plight upon arrival in the Shoddy Towns of 1956. At an age when I have not quite entered my spotty youth, and I am fresh from those rolling Cotswold Hills, I am confronted by phrases such as "Put t'wood in t'oil, will ta?" or "Sithee, lerrus gerr agate."

Careful questioning of my Batley Grammar School chums at play-times on the front yard began to unveil the esoteric mysteries of my new "lingua franca". I am soon talking like a Batley lad born and bred, so forty-five years later, there is little in the language to puzzle me. I must stress, however, that the meanings of phrases I have given here are my own interpretation of those yester-year explanations. Purists in matters of Shoddy Town Speak may wish to differ.

However, I still remain enthralled when I hear genuine Heavy Woollen District folk about their daily business. In that respect, I suppose I'm still a bit of a "comer-in". For those with a similar affliction, I include this short glossary of terms used in "Down the Ginnel" to complement that to be found in "Up the Snicket", as an aid to understanding our Shoddy Town twang. Long may it continue to enrich our daily lives with its colourful imagery and witty, down-to-earth humour.

***

Glossary

bahna   going to; expressing intent to carry out an action

bob   a shilling [twelve old pennies] In some instances, it can mean a violent blow. I first learned of its punning qualities when I heard Jack Hirst recite the following ditty during a Geography lesson in 1958:
"If your Bob dun't gie our Bob that bob as your Bob owes our Bob, our Bob'll gie your Bob a bob in t'ee."

bray   an act of violence, involving a blow of some kind. This may be a blow delivered either with a part of the anatomy or with an implement i.e. perhaps a fist or maybe a cricket bat

clart   cloth. In the plural form, I discovered at a young age that it can refer to a girl's knickers.

gerr agate   set about doing something. Alternatively, "agate" can be used to mean "in the act of doing something".

ginnel   a narrow passage-way between two solid, outdoor walls. In my understanding, its close compananion - a snicket - is a narrow passage-way between natural growth, such as hedges or bushes. Both represent handy places for adolescent naughtiness.

guzunder a large chamber-pot kept beneath the bed for instant nocturnal bladder relief. After use, it "goes under" from whence it came, to steam the winter nights away in the icy darkness.

half a dollar two shillings and sixpence; [current market value:$12^{1}/_{2}$p] in the form of a large, silver coin

kayli [pronounced kay-lie] Very sweet lemonade or sherbet crystals, in a variety of garish colours, sold in small conical paper-bags. Pure confectionery heaven to those of us who had experienced the pangs of sweet-rationing after the Second World War

maunt might not/must not. Often given as a warning: "Hey, tha maunt cheek thi father else tha'll gerra clout rahnd t'heead."

mesen The reflexive pronoun "myself". For a complete list of said pronouns, suitable for consumption by learned grammatical purists, please refer to "Up the Snicket".

nobbut	only, as in "'E's nobbut a bairn". We lads used the word as a noun to refer derogatively to anyone/ anything of a dimunitive, and thus unimportant, nature
pillock	a silly, useless person
Sat'day	the sixth day of the week, and in my time, the only day when proper football was played, kick-off at 3pm. At Batley Grammar School, it was our name for a punitive two hours in the Geography Room from 9.am until 11am
sly swaller	crafty intake of nicotine, usually taken either up a snicket or down a ginnel
spend	pocket-money given by kind, loving parents to their off-spring on Friday nights. Sadly, mine went almost entirely on Woodbines
wang	throw an object with some effort
wazzock	a very convenient term of abuse since its literal meaning has never been recorded in any learned etymological work.

***